NOLS
Wilderness
Navigation

NOLS
Wilderness
Navigation

SECOND EDITION

Darran Wells
illustrations by Jon Cox

STACKPOLE
BOOKS

Published by
STACKPOLE BOOKS
5067 Ritter Road
Mechanicsburg, PA 17055
www.stackpolebooks.com

Printed in the United States of America

10 9 8 7 6 5 4 3 2 1

Cover design by Caroline Stover
Cover photograph by Kyle Duba

*All illustrations by Jon Cox except as follows: 2, 102: The National Atlas of the United
States of America, United States Department of the Interior Geological Survey, 1970,
Courtesy of the University of Texas Libraries, The University of Texas at Austin; 3 (top
and bottom): iGage; 7: U.S. Geological Survey; 23, 107, 110, 112: U. S. Geological
Survey/Caroline Stover; 39: Caroline Stover; 104–5: Denis J. Dean, professor of geospatial
science, Colorado State University.*

Library of Congress Cataloging-in-Publication Data

Wells, Darran.
  NOLS wilderness navigation / Darran Wells ; illustrations by Jon Cox. —2nd ed.
    p. cm.
  Includes index.
  ISBN-13: 978-0-8117-1094-7 (pbk.)
  ISBN-10: 0-8117-1094-7 (pbk.)
 1. Orienteering—Equipment and supplies. 2. Navigation—Equipment and
supplies. 3. Outdoor recreation—Equipment and supplies. I. National Outdoor
Leadership School (U.S.) II. Title. III. Title: National Outdoor Leadership School
wilderness navigation.
  GV200.4.W45 2013
  796.58—dc23

                                                                    2012040324

Contents

Acknowledgments vii

Introduction ix

Chapter 1 Map Reading and Terrain Association 1

Chapter 2 Using a Compass 31

Chapter 3 Planning and Following a Route 66

Chapter 4 Altimeters 91

Chapter 5 Coordinate Systems 100

Chapter 6 GPS 116

Chapter 7 Lost in the Wilderness 133

Chapter 8 Digital Maps, Smartphone Apps, and Portable Power 151

Chapter 9 Competitive Navigation 172

Afterword 180

Appendix A: Where to Find Maps 183

Appendix B: Websites 184

Appendix C: Suggested Reading 185

Index 186

Acknowledgments

This book would never have been written without the support of the staff and students of the National Outdoor Leadership School. Particularly helpful were Drew Leemon, who shared his wisdom and feedback on the initial draft; Joanne Haines and Bruce Palmer, who shepherded the process along through the publication department; Jeanne Obrien, who helped build relationships and make connections with all of the navigation gadget manufacturers; and Adam Swisher, who helped with the final production and layout.

Amy Lerner at Stackpole Books has been great in getting things finalized and making sure balls were not dropped!

Jon Cox is just a great illustrator and all-around good guy. Thanks for your hard work making this book look good.

Ed Crothers of the AMGA shared a wonderful presentation on the secrets of USGS topo maps during the Association of Outdoor Recreation and Education Conference in San Antonio last year.

Many product manufacturers were open and helpful in sharing new technologies with me for this book. Special thanks to James Atkin and the Goal Zero team, the Creative Energies crew, Charlie Conly at Delorme, Ryan Perry at Brunton, Derek Moore at SPOT/Globalstar, Darwin Brown at ACR, and the team at Mophie.

Thanks to the wonderful faculty, staff, and students in the Outdoor Education and Leadership program at Central

Wyoming College for their suggestions, support, and time on this project.

Most of all I'd like to thank my wife, Stacy, and daughter, Willow, for their patience while I was sitting at the computer instead of climbing and hiking with them last spring.

Introduction

The reasons for venturing into the wilderness these days are countless. Glacial mountains, desert canyons, tropical jungles, and even arctic tundra can lift the burden of life in the city or suburbs. Wilderness travelers pursue everything from scientific study to conservation to sports and recreation. Whatever your reasons for leaving the pavement, good navigation skills will make your journey safer and more fun.

The National Outdoor Leadership School (NOLS) has been teaching wilderness navigation to novices and experts alike for more than forty years. With hundreds of professional field instructors drawing on past experience and a thorough knowledge of new technology, NOLS is able to provide the most complete and easy-to-follow land navigation curriculum available today.

How to Use This Book

Whether you are going for a day hike at a local state park, gearing up for a month-long climbing expedition, or learning to navigate for a multiday adventure race, this book is crafted to teach you to get yourself to your destination quickly and efficiently.

While there are other books on land navigation on the market, most are outdated and take a didactic approach: you are expected to learn by reading and by memorizing formulas. At NOLS, we have discovered that students learn to navigate best when they acquire skills sequentially and experientially. Learning to navigate well is more like learning to rock climb than learning to solve algebra problems. It requires that you go outside and practice. *NOLS Wilderness Navigation* gives you the tools and skills you need in a thoughtful sequence, and it walks you through practical field exercises to help you become a competent and confident navigator. It also uses a "light math" approach that minimizes math errors commonly made using other navigation techniques.

This book should not be read cover to cover in one sitting. If you are new to backcountry travel, it is important that you follow the sequence of skills carefully. You should achieve competency in the exercises at the end of each chapter before continuing, especially since some of these exercises contain new information that should not be overlooked. Expect to spend several hours or even several days in the field practicing the skills in each chapter before moving on to the next. As with many outdoor skills, practice makes perfect.

If you are a more experienced backcountry navigator, you can use this book as a reference or field guide to review topics of immediate interest. It is filled with tips to help you sharpen your skills with map, compass, altimeter, map software, and GPS. You will also find lists of resources, gear guidance, and useful websites in the back.

This book will not teach you how to plan your food rations, set up a camp, travel in winter, maneuver a sea kayak, explore caves, go horse-packing, climb rock and ice, or any number of other outdoor skills. For these, we suggest taking courses from professional instructors and consulting established reference works.

A Few Definitions

Before getting started, it's good to get a handle on some commonly confused jargon.

Navigation is the process of locating a destination and maintaining your direction as you travel toward it. Two important parts of navigation are orientation and routefinding.

Orientation is the process of determining exactly where you are located—knowing your position on the map and the land that it corresponds to—and in which direction you are facing. Successful navigators try to stay oriented at all times. You may be oriented without doing any navigating, but you can't navigate (at least not very well) without being oriented.

Orienteering is the sport of competitive cross-country navigation using a map and compass. See chapter 9 for more on orienteering.

Routefinding means choosing the most efficient path of travel for the group you are leading. Speed, safety, and energy conservation all determine efficiency, and the most efficient route may not be the shortest distance to your destination. Chapter 3 is devoted entirely to helping you become a good routefinder.

Before Hitting the Trail

If you haven't spent much time in the wilderness, a little planning and preparation can save you a lot of grief—it may even save your life. As you gain experience, you will become comfortable hiking, canoeing, or skiing greater distances away from civilization. Before you get too far down that trail, though, there are three important things you need to take care of:

1. *Take a course in wilderness first aid.*

   A good first aid kit is not much use in the wilderness without adequate first aid training.

2. *Leave a travel plan.*

You'll need to leave a detailed travel plan with a responsible adult before leaving on an expedition. See page 25 for specific guidance on writing and using travel plans.

3. *Pack essential gear.*

In addition to clothing and standard camping gear, there are several items you simply should not leave behind when you're heading away from roads and medical facilities and into the wilderness:

- Weatherproofed topo map(s)
- Compass
- Extra food
- Extra clothing
- First aid kit
- Lighter or weatherproof matches
- Multitool or knife
- Lined or weatherproof pack
- Headlamp
- Extra batteries
- Identification
- Medication or special medical equipment
- Water bottle or hydration system
- Means of water purification
- Sunglasses and sunscreen (especially when you're in snowy environments)

It is worth making a practice of always carrying this gear with you into the backcountry. Even on shorter trips, the extra weight will make you more fit. If this seems like a burden, consider that some of today's long-distance mountain runners will train by running marathon distances with these items in their packs!

Leave No Trace

The Leave No Trace Center for Outdoor Ethics is a national organization devoted to promoting responsible outdoor recreation. In coordination with NOLS and various land management agencies, it has developed seven principles to guide backcountry visitors to minimize their impact on the outdoors. Keep them in mind whenever possible so that you may help to preserve the wilderness for future visitors.

1. *Plan ahead and prepare.*
   Know the regulations and special concerns for the area you'll visit. Prepare for extreme weather, hazards, and emergencies. Schedule your trip to avoid times of high use. Visit in small groups, and split larger hiking parties into groups of four to six. Repackage food to minimize waste. Use a map and compass to eliminate the use of marking paint, rock cairns, or flagging.

2. *Travel and camp on durable surfaces.*
   Durable surfaces include established trails and campsites, rock, gravel, dry grasses, or snow. Protect riparian areas by camping at least 200 feet from lakes and streams. Good campsites are found, not made—do not alter a site to meet your needs. In popular areas, concentrate use on existing trails and campsites, walk single file in the middle of the trail (even when it's wet or muddy), keep campsites small, and focus activity in areas where vegetation is absent. In pristine areas, disperse your group to prevent the creation of campsites and trails, and avoid places where impacts are just beginning.

3. *Dispose of waste properly.*
   "Pack it in, pack it out" should be your mantra here. Inspect your campsite and rest areas for trash or spilled foods. Pack out all trash, leftover food, and litter. Deposit

solid human waste in catholes that are 6 to 8 inches deep and at least 200 feet from water, camp, and trails; cover and disguise them when finished.

Pack out toilet paper and hygiene products. To wash yourself or your dishes, carry water 200 feet away from streams or lakes and use small amounts of biodegradable soap. Scatter strained dishwater.

4. *Leave what you find.*

Preserve the past: examine, but do not touch structures and artifacts of cultural or historic significance. Leave rocks, plants, and other natural objects as you find them. Avoid introducing or transporting non-native species. Do not build structures or furniture or dig trenches.

5. *Minimize campfire impact.*

Campfires can cause lasting impact to the backcountry. Use a lightweight stove for cooking and a candle lantern for light. Where fires are permitted, use established fire rings, fire pans, or mound fires. Keep fires small. Only use sticks from the ground that can be broken by hand. Burn all wood and coals to ash, put out campfires completely, and scatter the cool ashes.

6. *Respect wildlife.*

Observe wildlife from a distance. Do not follow or approach animals. Never feed wildlife: it damages their health, alters their natural behaviors, and exposes them to predators and other dangers. Protect wildlife and your food by storing rations and trash securely. Control pets at all times, or leave them at home. Avoid wildlife altogether during the winter or when they are mating, nesting, or raising young.

7. *Be considerate of other visitors.*

Respect other visitors and protect the quality of their experience. Be courteous. Yield to other users on the trail, and step to the downhill side of the trail when encountering pack stock. Take breaks and camp away from trails and other visitors. Avoid loud voices and noises—let nature's sounds prevail.

A Few Final Words

As you build your navigation toolbox, beware of letting technology become a crutch. Keep the tool between your ears sharp and ask yourself what you would do if you lost your GPS, your compass, or even your map. As you learn to navigate on your own, you will be venturing into places where medical care is farther away and more difficult to reach than you have probably ever experienced. Hopping from rock to rock across a creek 10 miles from the nearest road should be given more consideration than jumping over a flowerbed in your front yard. Be conservative.

Until you are an expert at finding your way, you should not even consider going into the wilderness alone. While it's not always possible, a group of at least four is usually safest. If one gets hurt, two can go for help and one can stay with the injured person.

Finally, know and respect your group members' limitations. Have fun, but be safe!

CHAPTER 1

MAP READING AND TERRAIN ASSOCIATION

In this era of modern navigation devices, it is still true that the single most important skill for a navigator to have is the ability to read a map. Having the right map and knowing how to read it has made or broken countless trips to wild places. Regardless of your reasons for venturing into the wild, when you are lost, little else matters. On expeditions, navigators are often seen as heroes or fools depending predominantly on their ability to match their location on land to a point on the map.

The step-by-step skill progression in this chapter will help you to successfully navigate on your own. As you work through this chapter—and during your first few times in the field—leave the compass in your pocket or backpack, using it only in case of an emergency. You should start the learning process by studying the shape of the land itself. While some outdoor educators introduce map and compass together, NOLS instructors have found not only that students can navigate in many areas without using a compass at all, but that they develop their map reading skills faster without one. The more navigational toys you have to play with, the less you are focused on your surroundings.

As you begin to recognize distant land features by sight, you can start to compare them with what you see on your map. Only after you are comfortable associating the terrain with the images on the map should you begin to use your compass. More advanced gadgetry like altimeters and GPS receivers should not be added to your toolbox until much later, when you have mastered the basics of map and compass. In fact, if you learn to map-read well, you may be able to achieve all of your backcountry goals without electronics.

Finding the Right Map

Most of the maps you have probably seen are called planimetric maps. They show everything in one plane, as if the world is flat. Gas station road maps and atlases are planimetric. Two kinds of planimetric maps suited for planning trips to wilderness areas are recreation and guidebook maps. Recreation maps are printed by government agencies like the Bureau of Land Management and National Park Service for a specific use, such as mountain biking or horsepacking. Guidebook maps are intended to get you to a specific trail or land feature; some feature trail profile maps telling you how long and steep a trail will be. You can use

Planimetric map of the area near Lander, Wyoming

From top to bottom: more detailed topographic and topo relief maps of the area near Lander, Wyoming

these maps or a roadmap to plan where you will enter the wilderness. And for shorter trips on clearly marked trails, one of these may be all you need.

For trips into the wilderness, however, you will want a topographic map. Topographic maps depict the shape of the land (its topography) with what are known as contour lines. Each contour represents a specific elevation. By developing your ability to read contour lines and match them to features on the land, you can locate yourself in almost any place on earth. Contours are discussed more fully on page 12.

You may not be surprised to learn that there are different kinds of topo maps. The most important distinguishing feature of a topo is its scale. You can find topos in scales from 1:10,000 to 1:100,000 and up. Don't let the numbers scare you—they simply tell how much the map has been reduced. On a 1:24,000-scale map, one inch on the map represents 24,000 inches (0.4 mile) on land, and one foot equals 24,000 feet (4.5 miles). A large-scale map has a smaller number in its ratio (e.g., 1:24,000). It represents a smaller area but has more details. Large-scale maps are best for hiking, canoeing, or skiing. The smaller the map's scale, the larger the area it represents, and the more difficult it becomes to use for wilderness travel. (If you were hiking along in the woods for several days, your location wouldn't change much on a map of the entire United States, for instance.) Topo maps start to become difficult to use for land navigation when the scale gets below 1:100,000 (e.g., 1:250,000). The best scale for learning wilderness navigation is 1:24,000 or 1:25,000. In Alaska, you may be using a 1:63,360 map, where 1 inch equals 1 mile. In Europe and Canada, you will commonly find 1:50,000-scale maps, where 20 millimeters equals a kilometer.

In the United States, most backcountry travelers use United States Geological Survey quadrangle maps, known as quads. USGS quads are developed from aerial photographs, which are used to determine where the contour lines should appear. The

National Geographic Society, among others, produces a series of topo maps that feature shaded areas to give a three-dimensional view. While these "relief" maps help in identifying topography, they are rarely found in large scales.

If you travel in the backcountry often enough, there will come a time when you will need to read your map in the rain. Weatherproofing maps can be as simple or as complicated as you wish to make it. One easy method is to carry your maps in large plastic bags with zip tops. Ideally, they will be large enough to allow you to keep two to four folded maps together, for when you are traveling on the margins or corners of the maps. Disposable plastic bags are the lightest, and they are cheap and easy to replace when they get damaged. Use one bag for the map or maps you are currently on, and another to store the rest of your maps in an accessible place.

There are also several waterproofing laminates and specially designed map cases on the market. The laminates work well, but they make it difficult to write on the map in pencil. Some hikers prefer to use map cases that hang from their neck for easy access. If you're in a hurry, however, hanging cases can flop around and snag on heavy brush.

Reading a Topographic Map

There are good and bad times to develop your map-reading skills. A bad time would be when you are lost deep in the mountains alone at night during a blizzard—you might have trouble focusing on the task at hand. Initially, it is better to learn the basics in a comfortable setting where the likelihood and consequences of getting lost are low—your living room, for instance. While you certainly can't learn to recognize terrain features while indoors, you can become familiar with the signs and symbols on your map.

Basic Directions

You probably know that the four main cardinal directions are north, south, east, and west. As you can see on the compass rose below, they can be divided into northwest (NW), northeast (NE), southwest (SW), and southeast (SE). And those directions can be further broken down into north-northeast (NNE), east-northeast (ENE), east-southeast (ESE), south-southeast (SSE), south-southwest (SSW), west-southwest (WSW), west-northwest (WNW), and north-northwest (NNW).

Open a topo map and lay it out in front of you so that you can see the entire surface. The top of the map always faces north; in fact, on a USGS quad, the lines that make up the side margins are the only ones guaranteed to point toward true north. (See page 42 for a discussion of true north versus magnetic north.)

IN THE MARGINS

There are various useful tools and pieces of information located along the edges of topo maps. Expect the following elements on a USGS map:

The *name* of the quadrangle appears in both the upper and lower corners on the right side. The quad gets its name from a prominent land feature or population center located on the map. If you fold your map as shown in the illustration on page 8,

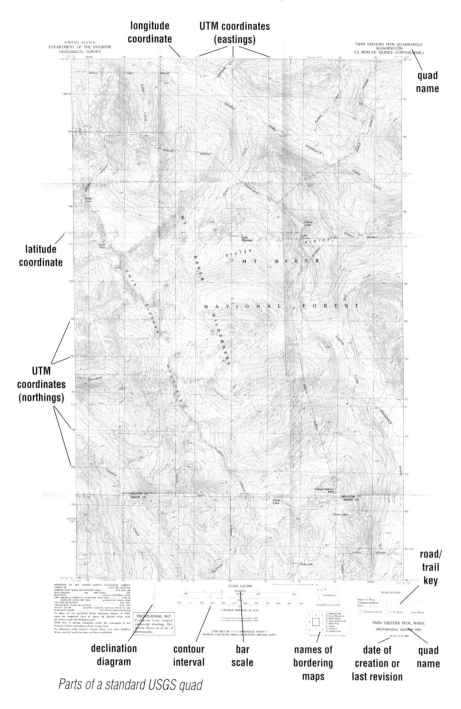

Parts of a standard USGS quad

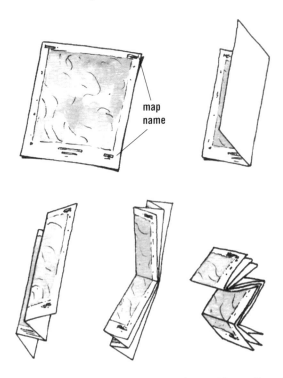

map
name

Fold your maps so that the map name can be read from either side.

you'll be able to read the name from either side; this makes searching through a pile of maps much easier.

The *date* the map was created or last revised is located below the name in the bottom right corner. While government agencies work to regularly update these quadrangles, they often cannot keep up with new trails and other features for every inch of North America. In some places, especially developing countries, a map made in the 1940s may be the most recent one available. Pay careful attention to the date of your map. The older the map, the more likely it is that glaciers have receded, ponds have dried up, trails and roads have moved, or things have otherwise changed.

The *bar scale* is located along the bottom center of the map. It consists of rulers that give distances in miles, feet, and kilometers.

Below the scale is the *contour interval*. This is the elevation difference between contour lines. On 1:24,000-scale USGS quads, the contour interval is usually 40 feet (12.19 meters). A contour interval of 50 feet (15.24 meters) or less will make it easier for you to learn to read contour lines. Contour intervals greater than 100 feet (30.48 meters) are rarely useful for foot travel outside very large mountain ranges like the Himalayas.

The *declination diagram* is located in the lower left. It consists of two vectors that indicate the differences between magnetic north (MN), true north (TN), and grid north (GN). These distinctions are explained in the sections on declination and GPS.

The numbers running along the edges of the map are *coordinates*. These are useful in giving your precise location over a radio or cell phone (e.g., for a helicopter evacuation) or when you are using GPS. Newer maps will have Universal Transverse Mercator (UTM) grid lines printed across the face of the map to assist in determining your coordinates.

Most quads will also feature a *key* titled "Highways and Roads" or "Road Classification" in the bottom right. This shows how roads and trails will be represented on the map.

The *names of bordering maps* appear in parentheses on every side and in the corners of older maps. Newer maps feature a diagram in the lower right showing the names of all the adjoining quads.

MAP COLORS

USGS maps all use the same color system. Look for examples of the following colors on the map you are using:

White indicates an area that is not forested. There may be snow, sand, boulders, tundra, sagebrush, or the occasional tree—anything other than dense forest or water. White doesn't automatically mean easy travel or great camping!

Green indicates vegetation. Solid green is a woodland forested area, defined by the USGS as having trees dense enough to conceal a platoon (around forty soldiers) in one acre. The border areas between green and white are often patchy and feature spotty tree coverage.

Blue means water. Solid blue shapes indicate lakes or ponds, while thick, continuous blue lines represent rivers. On older maps, dashed blue lines indicate seasonal streams, which run during the snowmelt in spring and early summer; newer maps use thin, solid lines. White areas covered with tiny blue shrubs and dashes mark seasonal marshes in a clearing. Marshes that are underwater year-round appear on a blue background. Springs show up as tiny blue squiggles and are often labeled "spring." Glaciers and permanent snowfields are enclosed by a dashed blue line. Blue is also used for contour lines on glaciers.

Black is used for names and human-made features—trails, dirt roads, boundaries, buildings, bridges, and mines. Black is also used for elevations that have been field-checked.

Red markings are reserved for US land survey lines, trail numbers, and major roads and boundaries. Many older US maps show red, numbered grid lines that are part of a survey system called "township and range." Today, few but foresters and surveyors use this grid system. It can be helpful in measuring linear distance since most of these grids are one square mile.

Purple is used for corrections or revisions that have been made to the original version of the map but have not been field-checked. Usually, the revisions will be dated on the bottom of the map.

Brown is reserved for contour lines and their elevations (except on glaciers).

Gray or *pink* areas indicate human developments and densely built-up areas such as towns or neighborhoods.

Measuring Distances

You can measure any distance on a map very accurately using only a string. Strings that do not stretch will work the best. A shoelace, piece of "parachute" cord, or the lanyard on your compass will work fine. Trails, particularly those in the mountains, seldom continue for very long in a perfectly straight line, and rulers, sticks, and fingers can't give accurate distances for long, winding paths.

By using a piece of string, you can determine the mileage for even the most winding trails.

To measure the distance between two points:

1. Place your map on a flat surface.
2. Keeping one end of your string on the start point, place the string along your planned route so that it follows it exactly.
3. Pinch the spot in the string where it intersects your destination.
4. Keeping that spot pinched between your fingers, stretch the string out along the scale at the bottom of the map to get your linear distance. You may have to move the string across the scale several times. Keep in mind that 1:24,000-scale quads have a scale that represents 2 miles in total length, but with a "0" in the middle and "1"s on either end.

Reading Contour Lines

Reading and understanding contour lines is the essence of map reading. While they may seem like a jumbled mess now, they will soon tell you volumes about the land you are traveling through. Contour lines are imaginary lines that run through areas of equal elevation. They may intersect but will never cross. If you were to follow the path of one on land, you would be walking at a constant elevation above sea level. The quintessential natural contour line is the shoreline of a lake.

The elevation difference between each line remains the same throughout a given map. This means that you can easily tell how steep an area is by how close together the contour lines are. Where the lines are spread far apart, the land is fairly flat. Where the lines are close together, it is steep. In a very flat area, like a desert, there may be only a few contour lines on the whole map. In a very steep, cliff-filled area, like Washington's North Cascades, there will be many contour lines crowded together.

Index contours are the heavier brown lines that include elevation numbers. On 1:24,000-scale quads, index lines are 200 feet apart in elevation. Between each pair of index contours are four light-brown lines that do not have elevations marked on them. These are known as intermediate contours, and they are usually 40 feet apart. The distance between any two successive contours is known as the contour interval.

Converging contours are contour lines that appear as one thick brown line. When contours converge, they indicate a cliff—vertical or near-vertical terrain. Unless you're going rock or ice climbing, avoid converging contour lines. Supplementary contours only appear in relatively flat terrain. These are dotted contour lines that mark the interval halfway between two intermediate lines.

Terrain Association

The ability to recognize land features by matching them to the contour line patterns on your map (and vice versa) is called terrain association. Terrain association is crucial to navigating with a topographic map. Good navigators are able to look at a map and see the entire route in their mind's eye. The best navigators can accurately describe exactly what an entire hiking day may look like to the rest of the folks in their party just by looking at the map. In this way, they can play an essential part in day-to-day planning. The following example shows just how much they can contribute to the process:

> *We shouldn't overdress starting out because we'll be heading up a steep hill in the morning sun. As the terrain levels out, we'll reach a plateau with a beautiful view of Angel Peak. We might want to take our first break and snap some photos there. We should also refill our water bottles at*

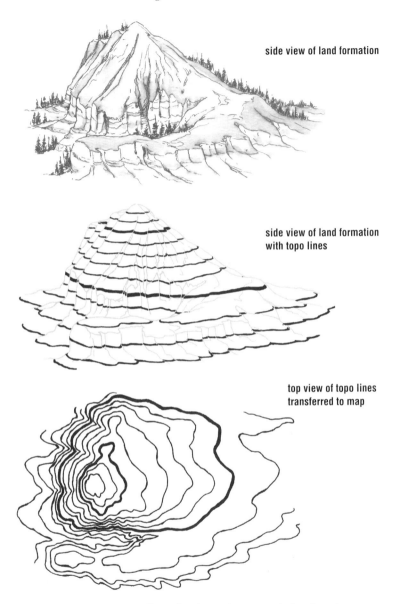

side view of land formation

side view of land formation with topo lines

top view of topo lines transferred to map

Contour lines allow a two-dimensional map to represent elevation changes. Notice the familiar shape of this particular land formation? You can achieve a similar effect by making a fist and drawing concentric circles around your knuckles—the view from above is like looking at a topo map.

the stream there before we head across the dry plateau. We should be descending into a shady, tree-filled valley to the north by noon. There may be patches of snow on that side. We'll drop down some steep switchbacks for an hour or so before popping out into a clearing on the valley floor where we'll have to cross a small river. We should all make sure the gear in our packs is waterproofed. There should be great camping in the meadow after we cross the creek. If we leave now, taking breaks and traveling at the pace we traveled yesterday, we should be in camp by 3:00 or 3:30.

Whether or not you are traveling in truly mountainous terrain, you should think of the land you are traveling on in terms of hills, drainages, and ridges. Being able to identify these three basic features by looking at the contour lines on your map will go a long way toward successful navigation. If you have a topo map handy, try to identify examples of each on your map.

A summit or peak is the highest point on any hill or mountain. A small circle surrounded by increasingly larger shapes usually indicates a summit—as they grow larger, elevation drops. Significant summits with verified elevations are often indicated on maps by a benchmark (marked "BM"), triangle, X, or elevation.

A ridge or spur is a relatively narrow area of elevation descending from a summit. It is the topographic opposite of a drainage. A ridge is indicated in contour lines by U shapes with the curve of the U pointing downhill.

A drainage or reentrant is any linear area where water would flow if it were poured on to the surface. There are countless names for the different kinds of drainages depending on their size and location. Gullies, couloirs, valleys, arroyos, crevasses, and canyons are all drainages. Drainages are indicated in contour lines by V shapes, where the apex of the V points uphill.

While mountains do have a general cone shape, their sides are textured by ridges and drainages. If you look at a large aerial

summit

ridge

drainage

saddle

depression

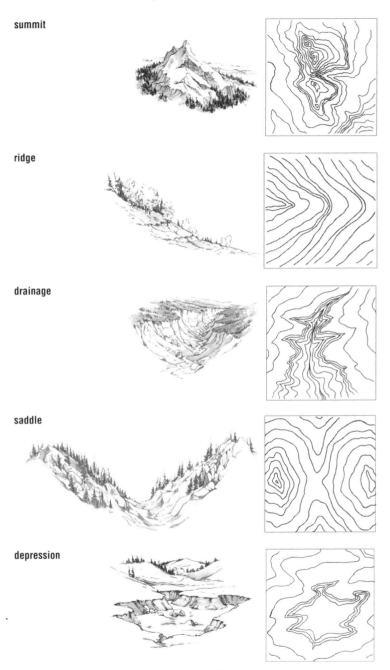

Contour patterns of common topographical features

photograph of virtually any mountain, you will probably see instances of both descending from the summit. They tend to alternate—ridge, drainage, ridge, drainage, and so on.

A saddle is a low point on a ridge between two summits. The contour lines of a saddle form an hourglass shape. Saddles are usually the easiest route from one side of a chain of hills to the other. There are many different kinds. In glaciated terrain, a saddle between two glaciers is called a col. Very steep and rocky saddles are sometimes called notches. Saddles large enough to drive a car through are called passes.

Once you develop an eye for land features, you will be able to look at a route and easily determine whether it ascends or descends the features it crosses. Until then, you can read the elevations on the index lines. Are the numbers going up or down?

Orienting Your Map without a Compass

To orient your map, you must turn it so that the cardinal directions on the map match those on land. An oriented map helps you determine your exact location and what lies between you and your destination. There are two ways to do this without a compass—using the sun and the stars or using terrain association. It's recommended that you practice both methods and learn to use them together whenever possible.

USING THE SUN AND STARS TO ORIENT YOUR MAP

You probably learned in grade school that the sun rises in the east and sets in the west. This is in essence true, though as the seasons change, the points where the sun crosses the horizon gradually shift. Nonetheless, you should be able to roughly orient your map using the sun alone, particularly at dawn and dusk.

In the middle of the day, you can use a different technique to determine north. In the northern hemisphere, the sun does

In the northern hemisphere at midday, the shadows of vertical objects will point north.

not cross directly overhead as it does at the equator. It actually passes just to the south. (This is the reason you find more shade and snow on the north faces of North American mountains.) Because of this, the shadow of a perfectly straight tree points north at midday, i.e., the moment exactly halfway between sunrise and sunset for that time of the year—it's usually between noon and 2:00 PM. The length of this shadow will vary depending on your location. The farther north of the equator you are, the longer the shadow. At the equator, there is no shadow at all, and in the southern hemisphere, of course, the shadow points south.

You can also find north at night if you can see the stars. In the northern hemisphere, it's as simple as finding the Big Dipper. Look for the two stars at the end of this familiar constellation, the ones that lie farthest from the handle. They form a straight line that points directly toward Polaris, which is known as the North Star because it always lies directly to the north. On a clear night in the northern hemisphere, you can hardly miss Polaris: it is a bright star that stands alone, and as the night progresses, the other stars will appear to revolve around it. The farther north you are, the higher it will appear in the sky, and the more difficult it will be to tell which direction is north.

In the southern hemisphere, Polaris may be too low on the horizon to be seen, and there is no "South Star" over the South Pole. In places such as southern Chile or New Zealand, the

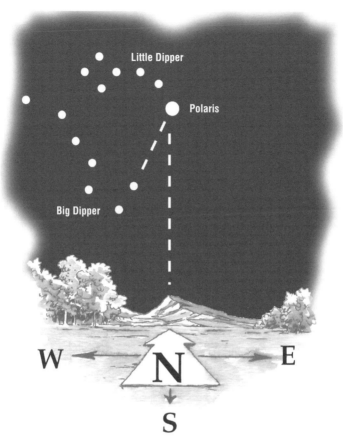

You can use the Big Dipper to locate Polaris, the North Star.

Southern Cross is often used for direction. It is a smaller constellation (less than half the size of the Big Dipper) and actually looks more like a kite than a cross, because it lacks a bright star in the middle. If you draw an imaginary line along the long beam of the cross and another one from the two "Pointer Stars" near the Cross, the intersection marks true south.

(Note: Traveling at night can be a magnificent experience, but it is considerably more difficult and dangerous than traveling during the day. It is the domain of expert navigators. Don't

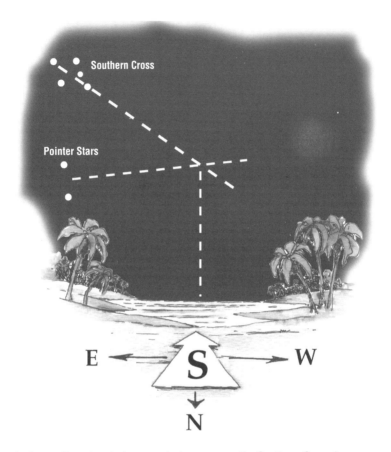

In the southern hemisphere, navigators can use the Southern Cross for guidance.

consider it unless you are in easy terrain or are with experienced people. See pages 83–84 for tips on nighttime travel.)

USING TERRAIN ASSOCIATION TO ORIENT YOUR MAP

Unfortunately, the sun and stars are not always visible when we need them. While you are learning navigation, you should think of them the way you will come to think of your compass—as a tool to verify that you have oriented your map correctly using terrain association. The first step in terrain association is to locate a nearby terrain feature that is easy to find on your map. Linear features such as trails, ridges, and drainages are best. If you can't find a land feature that you can positively match to contour lines, you can't orient your map with terrain association alone. Next, rotate your map until the shape on the map is aligned with the terrain feature you can see. Then verify that the map is oriented correctly. Take a look around to make sure that the positions of what you see on land match those on the map, and that the cardinal directions correspond to shadows cast by the sun.

Estimating Steepness

The measurement of a hill's steepness is called the slope angle. If you are traveling in the mountains, you may need to determine the slope angle to decide whether or not to follow a particular route. An angle from 0 to 5 degrees is fairly easy; you may not even notice that it is slightly inclined. From 5 to 25 degrees, you will certainly know you're going uphill. Slopes above 15 degrees will take more time to travel upon than flat terrain, which you should factor into your route planning. A moderate slope (25–35 degrees) can be a significant challenge, particularly if you are traveling off-trail with a backpack. The higher risk of falls and difficulty of travel on steep slopes (45+ degrees) should be reserved for those with mountaineering training. A 90-degree slope, of course, is a vertical wall or cliff.

A warning: on slopes over 35 degrees, you should start to be concerned with falling rocks. The safest way to deal with steep, rocky slopes is to avoid them. If you must ascend one, keep your group close together and follow a zigzag pattern on the way up to minimize the chance of someone knocking rocks down on to those below. And before you even think about climbing a snowy slope of more than 25 degrees, you should learn how to use an ice axe and assess avalanche danger from a trained professional. If in doubt, avoid steep terrain all together.

As you travel in mountainous terrain with your map, you will develop an eye for how steep a hill is by looking at contour lines. The closer the contours are to each other, the steeper the hill. There are several ways to get a more precise idea of how steep a slope may be. The easiest is by using a slope gauge. This navigational tool is designed for a given scale (e.g., 1:24,000) and provides the slope angle for a series of contour lines. Using a slope gauge when you're starting out will also help develop your eye for terrain association. You can find one at an outdoor retailer or online.

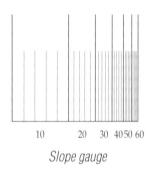

Slope gauge

To determine the slope angle using a slope gauge:

1. Make sure the scale of the gauge matches the map scale.
2. Draw a straight line along the route you plan to take up the hill.
3. Move the gauge along the line until a section of the gauge aligns with the contours at the steepest part of your route. The index lines should overlap precisely.
4. The number indicated on the gauge is the slope angle for that part of the hill.

If you are a math geek or just prefer to have more factors to consider when planning routes, you may be interested in the grade of the slope. If you've driven in the mountains, you've probably seen road signs warning of a steep grade. The grade is the change in height of a slope divided by its distance (as the crow flies, not the distance on the ground), rendered as a

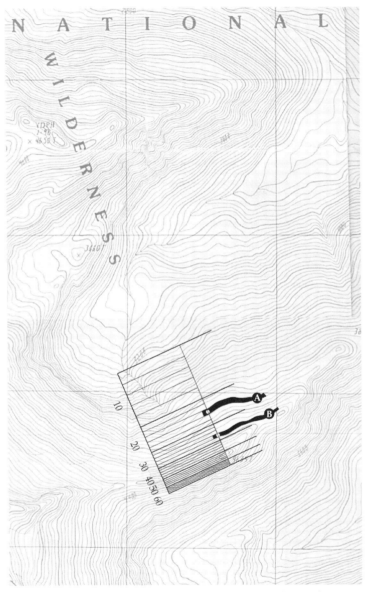

A slope gauge allows you to measure the slope angle at a given point on a topo map. The point along contour "A" has a slope angle of 20 degrees; the point along contour "B" has an angle of 30 degrees.

percentage. For a slope that covers a distance of 400 feet and drops 100 feet, the grade is 25 percent. A slope 400 feet long and 400 feet high has a grade of 100 percent (45 degrees). As a general rule, you should avoid slopes where the height is equal to or greater than the distance unless you are mountaineering.

Total Elevation Gain

Measuring the elevation you will gain on a particular route before starting out allows you to estimate how much time and energy you will expend. Measuring elevation is as simple as counting contour lines. Be careful, however, not to count the lines where you are losing elevation. While you are learning to identify map features, it may help to double-check by looking at the elevation of each contour line. Are the numbers increasing or decreasing as you travel along your route?

At first glance, it may be tempting to simply add or subtract the elevation change between your origin and final destination. However, this will not give you an accurate idea of what your travel time may be. It is all those ups and downs you encounter during your hiking day that will slow you down. For example, if you start on the North Rim of the Grand Canyon and want to travel to the South Rim (ending the day at nearly the same elevation), you cannot neglect the close to 1 mile of elevation you will have to regain as you climb back out of the canyon. If you ignored the elevation gain, your travel time would be off by at least six hours—try explaining that mistake to your exhausted hiking partners as you crawl up to camp in the dark! A hike such as this might actually need to be broken into two or three days.

The following guidelines are estimates based on typical speeds for an average party:

- 1,000 feet of elevation gain = time and effort of 1 additional mile; 200 meters of elevation gain = time and effort of 1 additional kilometer.
- 2 miles (about 3 k) on flat trail with full expedition backpacks takes approximately 1 hour.
- 1 mile (about 1.5 k) of off-trail travel with a full expedition pack takes approximately 1 hour.

Exercise 1. Writing a Travel Plan

A travel plan is an itinerary that gives an overview of your intended route. It carefully walks the reader through your route step by step. There are at least three good reasons to take the time to write a travel plan:

1. The process of writing a travel plan forces you to practice critical map reading skills as you plan your route,
2. A well-written travel plan can serve as a tool for you to monitor your route progress and stay on track while you are in the field,
3. A good travel plan can help someone find you in an emergency.

Unlike many of the exercises in this book, you can (and should) write a travel plan *before* going into the field. Make sure your plan includes the following details:

- The names of each person in your party and what equipment they are carrying. Identify important roles such as expedition leader, navigator, climbing leader, and so on.
- Your planned origin and destination for each day of your trip. Be as precise and descriptive as you can. If your destination is not right next to an obvious land feature, include directions and distances to three recognizable

features. Ask yourself if you would be able to find your location if someone just handed you this description.

- A detailed route description using named map features and cardinal directions.
- Time/distance calculations. Travel plan or not, every good navigator should be able to make these calculations.

  a. The linear distance from your origin to your destination.

  b. The perceived distance between origin and destination, which adds 1 mile per 1,000 feet of elevation gain.

  c. The moving travel time in hours, as determined by dividing the perceived distance (in miles or kilometers) by your party's average rate of travel (in miles or kilometers per hour).

  d. The total travel time, which is moving travel plus time for breaks, river crossings, and any other expected delays added in.

  e. The estimated time of arrival (ETA): your estimated time of departure (ETD) plus your total travel time.

- Contingency plans and information. These include alternate campsites and rendezvous points, anticipated hazards and obstacles, and potential causes for delay (which need to be factored in to your ETA as well). This information should be more detailed in situations where there are more hazards or unknowns that might prevent you from reaching your destination.

SAMPLE TRAVEL PLAN
Lake Lunker Fly-Fishing Expedition—Day 2 (8/9/2013)

1. **Team Members:** Missy White (expedition leader)—cookware and stove; Scott Kane—rain fly and tent poles; Stacy Wells—tent body, bear spray, and GPS; Dave Glenn—maps, compass, and first aid kit.

2. **Point of Origin:** ½ mile south of Lake Watonga, ⅔ mile northeast of the summit of Mt. Kalamazoo, and 1½ miles southwest of the Snake River at 10,200 ft.

   Destination: The north shore of Lake Lunker between Trail 456 and Big Lunker Creek.

3. **Route Description:**

   Leg 1: Leave camp hiking SE on the Highline trail. Climb switchbacks to intersection of Highline and Trail 456, gaining 900 ft. of elevation.

   Leg 2: Hike south on Trail 456 for 4½ miles, passing on the east side of Mt. Kalamazoo, handrailing Big Lunker Creek, and descending 350 ft. to intersection of Big Lunker and Small Lunker Creeks.

   Leg 3: Cross SL Creek and head SSW off trail, gaining 100 ft. for ¼ mile up a forested slope to destination at 10,950 ft.

4. **Time/Distance Calculations:**

   A. 6½ miles of linear distance.

   B. 6½ miles + 1 mile (1000 ft. of elevation gain) = 7½ miles perceived distance.

   C. 7½ miles ÷ 2 miles per hour = 3¾ hours of travel time.

   D. 3¾ hours + 1 hour (lunch, water breaks, and creek crossing) = 4¾ hours total time.

   E. 9:30 AM departure time + 4¾ hours = 2:15 PM ETA.

5. **Contingency Plans**

   If Small Lunker Creek is too fast or big to cross, we will camp in the small meadow ¼ mile north of the intersection of Big and Small Lunker Creeks.

Write travel plans for your next few trips into the backcountry, or for an imaginary trip based on your USGS quads. For the purposes of this exercise, choose an area that is familiar. You will gain a lot from writing a plan even for short day trips. Spend a day navigating entirely using your travel plan rather than reading your map. Are you able to find your way following the directions you've written?

Exercise 2. Practicing Terrain Association

The most important navigation skill to develop is your ability to recognize land features and associate them with the contour lines you see on your map. If you are unable to consistently recognize the difference between a drainage and a ridge or a saddle and a bowl, you are hopelessly bound to traveling on trails. Worse yet, even judging your location on a particular trail will be difficult unless you are standing at a trail intersection with accurate signs. This exercise will help you develop your eye for land features without even breaking a sweat.

First, find an area to visit with a good view. Choose a location that is high and clear of anything that would block your view—a hilltop, a high roadside pullout, a ridge, or even a rooftop in a hilly, rural area. For learning purposes, it's best to find a place where there are big, recognizable land features—like mountains, hills, or valleys or smaller drainages—that will be visible from one spot. The farther you can see, the better. A place you are familiar with is best.

Make sure you have topo maps that will cover all of the area you can see from your vantage point. In places that happen to fall near map edges or corners, you may need up to four maps. For this exercise, you will also need some blank white paper or a sketch pad, pencils, a writing surface, and about forty-five minutes. A camp chair, binoculars, and colored pencils are nice if you have them.

Once you are in the right spot with the right materials, orient your map. Rocks on the corners work well as paperweights to keep it from blowing away. Find your location and mark it on the map. Then take ten or fifteen minutes to study the map and identify as many corresponding land features as you can.

The next step is to put the real map away and try to sketch your own topo map based on the land features you see. Start your hand-drawn map by drawing any visible drainages and roads. Try to draw them to the same scale as your printed map by looking at the land—don't peek at the map! Then, mark the location of all the summits you can see.

You are now ready for the contour lines. If you are in a mountainous area, try to draw in just the index contours (every 200 feet on a 1:24,000 scale map). Take your time and try to be as accurate as possible. Start from summits and draw the consecutive contours that descend from them. Try to represent all the visible ridges, drainages, and bodies of water. Use binoculars if you have them.

Once you have finished your sketch, reorient your printed map and compare the same area to your drawing. Obviously, the level of detail and precision will not be the same, but try to determine where there are major differences. Do the contour lines form the same basic shapes and patterns? How accurate is the scale of your map? What about the distances between features?

As you learn to read topo maps, you should start to see the contour lines in your mind's eye as you look at the landscape. Try this exercise again after you've spent some time reading topos in the field.

Conclusion

Learning to read maps well takes practice, and there is no better way to practice than by being in the wilderness for an extended period of time. That means more time for you to get out and climb, bike, hunt, fish, bird-watch, backpack, or do whatever you love to do in the backcountry. It is normal to struggle and make

mistakes sometimes. Those who say they've never been disoriented or gone off route probably haven't challenged themselves
much. Navigating off-trail may be frustrating, but it will force you
to develop your map skills. (Before jumping in over your head,
however, read chapter 7 about how to avoid getting truly lost.)

The bottom line is: don't get discouraged if you have trouble
the first few times out. That's normal. Be patient and stick with
it. You will soon develop an eye for wilderness terrain that will
last you a lifetime.

CHAPTER 2 | USING A COMPASS

Imagine that you've spent an exciting weekend in the mountains and are headed back to the trailhead when you get caught in the dark. You've been traveling off-trail and there are several trails in the area. When you finally reach one, you're not really sure whether it's the right one and if it is, whether you should go left or right. While you could look for terrain features during the day to orient yourself, you simply can't see past the light of your headlamp, and the stars are covered by clouds.

A case such as this shows the limitations of navigating by sun, stars, and terrain alone. Anytime you find yourself in featureless terrain (desert, grasslands, tundra) or low-visibility situations (dense trees, fog, a whiteout), these methods become very difficult and the compass may be your only way to stay on track. Once you have spent a few days in the field with a topo map and gained a foundation in map reading, it is time to add a compass to your navigation toolbox. In this case, after trying to orient your map by memory, you would double-check your position with a compass and hopefully find that you are only a little off. Then, as you started down the trail, you would use the compass to verify the trail direction and arrive at the trailhead in no time.

A compass is a fantastic instrument, but, as with GPS and other tools, becoming too dependent on it too early can inhibit your development as a navigator. If you travel in the backcountry long enough, you might lose or break your compass at some

A Brief History of the Compass

Somewhere in the fog of history, humans discovered two things: the Earth has magnetic properties, and a rock called magnetite or lodestone responds to those properties. Historians generally agree that the Chinese made the first compasses some time around the eleventh century. Primitive, early versions consisted of a piece of lodestone resting on a cork in a bowl of water. In 1295, Marco Polo brought the compass back to Europe from the court of Kubla Khan. By 1400, the pivot compass was standard on British ships. Modern handheld compasses have really evolved very little since the fifteenth century. In the twentieth century, Swedish-born Bjorn Kjellstrom made some refinements, and by 1933 he had combined a protractor and magnetic needle to create the basic field compass we use today.

point and will need to know alternative techniques. Be sure you know how to find your way in easy-to-read terrain without a compass.

Use it only to double-check your map skills the first few times in the field, and you will gradually develop your eye for terrain association. (On thirty-day NOLS courses in the Wyoming Rockies, students usually navigate for the first week or two with maps alone.) Knowing when you really need to use a compass and when it is just a crutch will come with time.

Parts of a Compass

A compass is simply a device that responds to the Earth's magnetic fields by pointing to magnetic north, which is near Ellesmere Island, Canada (see page 42 for more details). All the plastic, rulers, numbers, and arrows are there to make a compass

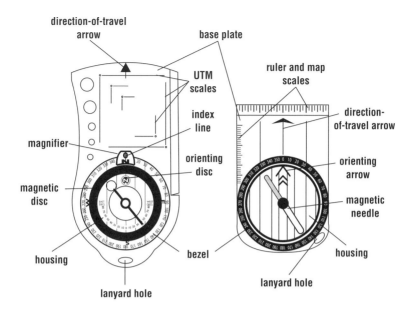

direction-of-travel arrow

base plate

ruler and map scales

UTM scales

index line

magnifier

direction-of-travel arrow

orienting disc

orienting arrow

magnetic disc

magnetic needle

housing

bezel

housing

lanyard hole

lanyard hole

Parts of basic disc and needle compasses

easier to use, but its essence is its north-pointing magnet. When used properly, it can help you to determine cardinal directions from almost any location on the planet.

The illustrations here and on page 35 show compasses with various basic and advanced features. At the very least, your compass must have a needle, bezel, and base plate. If you plan on traveling in the backcountry regularly or if you need a high level of precision (to compete at orienteering, for example), it is well worth investing in a more advanced compass. If you already own a compass, pull it out now and see if you can identify the following parts:

NEEDLE

The needle, which is made of magnetized iron, balances on a pivot so that it can swing easily in any direction. The north-seeking end of traditional compass needles is red; some also have a convenient glow-in-the-dark stripe. Some Brunton brand compasses use an all-black needle with a hollow circle on the north-seeking end for improved accuracy.

HOUSING AND BEZEL

The housing is the plastic liquid-filled vial that surrounds the needle. The needle is in a nonfreezing damping liquid so that the needle doesn't move erratically or freeze in subzero temperatures. The bezel is the rotating dial around the housing. The bezel (also called an azimuth ring) is marked with 360 degrees, usually in 2-degree increments. As you turn the bezel, you turn the entire housing. On the bottom of the housing on most compasses are meridian lines and an orienting arrow. The meridian lines can help you determine declination. On most compasses, the orienting arrow looks like a tiny shed that outlines the needle. Instead of the orienting arrow, some Brunton compasses have a targetlike orienting circle that adds precision. In both cases, the orienting shape on the base plate is used to outline or "box" the magnetic needle when determining your bearing or direction of travel.

BASE PLATE

The base plate is the rectangular piece of plastic on which the housing is mounted. It is often transparent and marked with rulers or UTM grid readers. It is also marked with a direction-of-travel arrow that, along with the orienting arrow on the bottom of the housing, helps you take and follow bearings. The end of this arrow that is closest to the azimuth ring is called the index line; this is where bearings are read.

SIGHTING MIRROR

Sighting mirrors are small mirrors that fold over the top of the housing to close the compass. Compasses with sighting mirrors

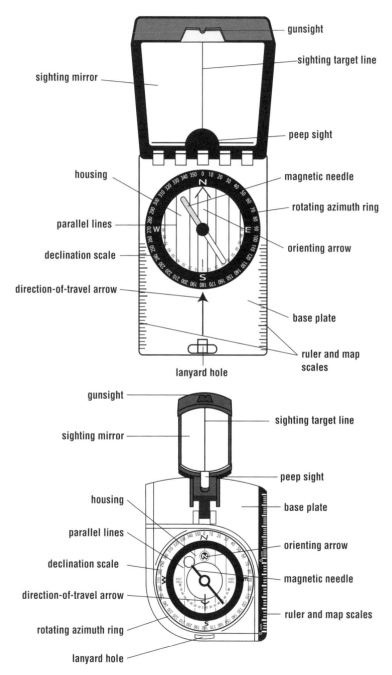

Parts of advanced compasses

are sometimes called prismatic compasses. They are used to more precisely align the compass with distant objects when taking or following a bearing. The advantage of the mirror is that it allows you to adjust the azimuth while sighting a distant object. Tilting the mirror toward you enables you to view the reflection of the orienting arrow while holding the compass at eye level and an arm's length away. This adds a significantly higher level of accuracy when using bearings. While most sighting mirrors cover the entire base plate when closed, some newer compasses use a lower profile mirror to allow a better view of your objective and more accurate sighting.

LANYARD

This is a fancy name for the cord attached to the base plate. Many lanyards have a sliding plastic toggle of some sort that can be used to measure distance on a map. While most folks use the toggle and lanyard to wear the compass around their necks when it's not in use, beware that the lanyard can occasionally catch on thick brush or climbing gear.

DECLINATION ADJUSTMENT

Many compasses feature an adjustable orienting arrow. This allows you to set the declination on your compass so that you do not have to add or subtract in the field while switching between magnetic and true bearings—a welcome convenience after an exhausting day in the mountains. Some compasses with a declination adjustment have a tiny screwdriver attached to the lanyard for turning the declination screw on the back of the bezel. Others may be adjusted without a screwdriver by pinching and rotating the housing while holding the azimuth ring still.

GLOBAL PIVOT

Ignore this advanced feature unless you are planning to use your compass outside North America. A global pivot allows the needle to tilt vertically in such a way that it is not affected by the Earth's different magnetic dip zones. (See the diagram on page 39.)

CLINOMETER

Some compasses have a second free-moving needle attached to the pivot inside the bezel. This nonmagnetic arrow is usually black and is used to measure the angle of a slope in the field when the compass is tilted on its side. This is a critical tool for those needing to assess avalanche potential.

MAGNIFYING GLASS

Even if your vision is good, it is occasionally nice to have a small magnifying glass built in to the base plate for reading tiny names and map features.

Types of Compasses

Special compasses are used in a wide variety of outdoor endeavors. There are specialized compasses for sea kayaking, sailing, adventure racing, and caving, just to name a few. New digital compasses are appearing on the market every day. While many compasses will perform some of the functions you need for backcountry travel, only base-plate compasses can meet all your navigational needs.

There are many different base-plate compasses to choose from. Simple models are less expensive but lack sighting mirrors, declination adjustments, and other special features. While they are adequate for land navigation in most areas, they mean you have to do a little more work or mental arithmetic if you are traveling exclusively on bearings—a possibility if you will be in the backcountry a lot. There are also compasses that feature a mirror but no declination adjustment, or vice versa.

Advanced or full-featured compasses are the best for wilderness navigation. If you are new to backcountry travel, paying for mirrors, lanyards, and clinometers might seem like a waste. If you have yet to purchase a full-featured compass, read the rest of this chapter and then decide whether the extra expense is worth it. Reliable compass manufacturers include Brunton, Silva, and Suunto.

A number of watches and smartphones now feature digital compasses. While digital compasses are becoming more accurate, they should still be seen as a backup tool and not a replacement for old-fashioned analog base-plate compasses. Watches are more difficult to accurately sight with and are almost useless for taking bearings from a map. This is not to say that they don't have their place in the backcountry, however—many of them also feature very accurate altimeter-barometers, which we will discuss more in chapter 4.

If you intend to use a digital compass to navigate, or even if there is a chance you might use it, be sure that it is calibrated properly and that the declination is set correctly. Most digital compasses are much easier to calibrate at home than in the field. If you're not sure if yours is calibrated correctly, compare it to an analog compass.

Digital watch compass

Using a Map and Compass Outside North America

If you will be traveling in wilderness areas in other countries, there are some important things to know. For one, you will not always find maps with the level of detail and scale available here in North America. Topographic maps of a 1:24,000 or 1:25,000 scale are rare in many developing countries, where you can often only find maps of 1:100,000 scale. Also remember that most countries of the world use metric (meters, kilometers) rather than statute (feet, miles) units of measurement for distance and elevation.

You may need a different compass as well. The Earth's magnetic fields pull compass needles not only in cardinal directions, but also up and down. Generally, the farther north you go, the more your needle will want to point down; the farther south you

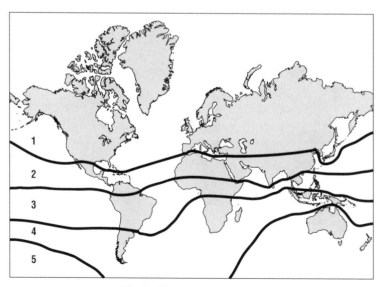

The Earth's magnetic dip zones

go, the more it will point up. This phenomenon is called compass dip. If the dip is too great, the needle will drag on the top or bottom of the housing and will not spin freely. Compass makers divide the Earth into several magnetic dip zones and balance compass needles differently for each zone. Therefore, a compass purchased up in Ontario may not be the ticket to helping you find that volcano down in Fiji. Contact your compass manufacturer directly to make sure your compass will work in the zone to which you are headed. As mentioned earlier, you can purchase a compass with a global pivot that is uniquely balanced to work in any magnetic dip zone. Wherever you go, be sure to double-check that your compass works well in a local town before heading into the backcountry.

Potential Problems for Compass Users

Imagine that you are leading an early-season expedition across a high alpine mesa in a blizzard. You have been hiking in deep snow for over eight hours, visibility is down to about 10 feet, and some members of your party are starting to show signs of hypothermia. There is only one place on the mesa where you can hike down, and you will have to travel due south on a bearing for several miles to reach it. You face what you believe to be south and double-check the direction with the compass. Several hard-fought hours later, arriving at a massive cliff, you check your map and realize that you've brought the entire expedition about two miles off-course to the southwest. You now still have two more miles to hike to get to camp, and some of your exhausted teammates are discussing pushing you off the cliff.

What happened? Could there have been magnets sewn into your jacket? The idea would seem ridiculous if it hadn't happened to me personally. Unfortunately, the designers of my fancy shell jacket (a gift!) chose to use magnets rather than Velcro to seal the zipper's storm flap. I could have faced any direction and believed I was headed south, since the magnetic end of the needle would always point toward me.

While a compass might not run out of batteries, there are still things that can go wrong. Much of the human-made gadgetry we carry around is magnetized. The easiest way to avoid falling prey to user compass errors is to always double-check yourself. Better yet, have someone else double-check you. In any group outing, there should be at least two people working on navigation. Part of learning to be a good navigator is explaining your decisions and encouraging your teammates to challenge them.

For those traveling to higher elevations or colder climates, it is common for a vacuum bubble to form within the compass housing. This occurs because the damping fluid contracts faster than the tightly sealed housing. The bubble should not affect the compass performance, and should disappear completely when you return to warmer temperatures. If the bubble does not disappear after a day or two, however, you could have a leak in the housing seal and a broken compass.

On the other end of the temperature spectrum, extreme heat can ruin a compass rather quickly. If the plastic itself doesn't melt, the liquid may overexpand and break the housing. Try not to leave the compass in direct sunlight for long in hot environments.

Just as they can ruin watches and other plastic navigational tools, chemicals can also ruin your compass. DEET, found in many insect repellents, is a common culprit in dissolving the ink off your compass and possibly eating through the housing. Be very careful when handling any potentially harmful substances.

Declination

Unless disrupted by magnets nearby, a magnetic compass needle will point to the Earth's northern magnetic pole. Contrary to popular belief, however, this is not the geographic North Pole. Magnetic north is currently located in the northern Canadian Arctic near Ellesmere Island. Most scientists agree that the Earth's magnetism is primarily an effect of movements in the Earth's outer molten core. As the molten core changes, so does the position of magnetic north. Magnetic north is now moving about 40 miles per year toward Siberia. In the United States and Canada, declination has historically moved several degrees east or west over many years before swinging back like a pendulum.

For ease of discussion, let's just say that your compass needle points to Ellesmere Island. The only thing you need to know to understand declination is that your compass needle points to Ellesmere Island instead of the North Pole. Declination is just the angular difference between the two. If you imagine a triangle with you, the North Pole, and Ellesmere Island as its three corners, the angle at your corner of the triangle would be the declination.

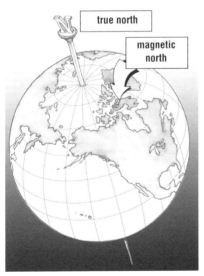

true north

magnetic north

Your declination changes depending on where you happen to be. If you are in Wisconsin, Illinois, or Mississippi, your declination is close to zero, and you may not need to set your declination at all. If you are in Seattle, your decli-

The needle of a compass does not point to the North Pole but to a point near Ellesmere Island, Canada.

nation is about 19 degrees east, while in New York the declination is about 15 degrees west, a tremendous difference.

To adjust precisely for declination, you must use the declination diagram in the bottom left on your topo map. Ignore the magnetic needle during this process; you are only concerned with adjusting the bezel correctly. Start with the bezel set to north, so that it reads 0 degrees at the index line. Lay the compass over the declination diagram so that the star (representing the North Pole) is under the N on the bezel. Then, holding the base-plate still, rotate the bezel until the orienting arrow is pointing to the "MN" on the diagram.

As a rule, if you are east of the 0 degree declination line, you will turn your bezel counterclockwise; if you are to the west, you

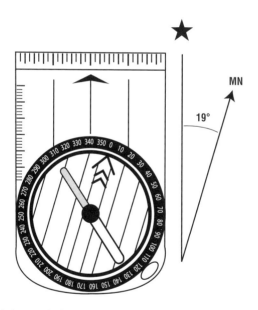

All USGS quads have a declination diagram that will allow you to reconcile magnetic north with true north. Simply place your compass over the diagram, matching the direction-of-travel arrow to true north and the orienting arrow to magnetic north.

will turn it clockwise. Declination is given in degrees east or west. Thus, although your index line will read 341 degrees in Seattle, the declination will be 19 degrees east. Folks with basic compasses may choose to mark their declination with a small, triangular piece of colored tape on the base plate. This is well worth doing if you will be traveling in one general area for an extended period of time, as it will help you to turn the bezel in the right direction. If you are confused about which way to turn the dial, simply place your compass over the declination diagram again.

If you have a compass with a declination adjustment feature (Suunto or Silva), you will adjust it by turning the tiny screw on the back of the bezel with a tiny screwdriver on your lanyard. Brunton compasses are adjusted by holding the bezel with one hand while pinching and rotating the housing with the other. In either case, the N on the azimuth ring should still be at the index line, while the orienting arrow should point to the correct declination. If your compass features a dial for adjusting declination on the back of the bezel, remember when you turn it over that in the West you are dealing with east declination and vice versa.

Remember that not only is magnetic north constantly changing, but the rate of change has been increasing in the last decade. If your map is more than five years old, the declination may be off a little. For areas in the United States, visit www.USGS.gov to get the most current declination in the area you will be visiting.

Boxing the Needle

After setting your declination, you can use your compass to face true north. You accomplish this by boxing the needle—moving

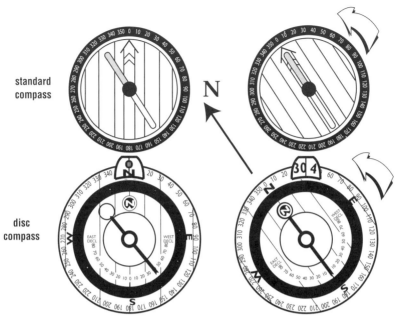

Boxing the needle

the compass until the magnetic end of the needle is outlined by the orienting arrow. There are two ways to box the needle: by holding the base plate still while turning the bezel, and by rotating the entire compass (base plate and all) without touching the bezel. Try them both a few times to make sure you understand the difference.

The second method is the one you want for finding true north. Set the compass declination and then box the needle by rotating the entire compass. The direction-of-travel arrow on the base plate is now pointing to true north. Pick the compass up and hold it in front of you, perpendicular to your chest, while the needle is boxed and the declination is set. You are now facing true north.

Orienting a Map with Your Compass

As discussed in chapter 1, orienting a map to the land features around you using terrain association is the best way to practice your map-reading skills. You should try to orient your map to the land every time you look at it in the field. Nonetheless, it's vital that you know how to use a compass to double-check your orientation or to orient the map when you cannot see land features.

First, set your declination correctly for your current location. Then lay your map on a flat surface or hold it so that it is level.

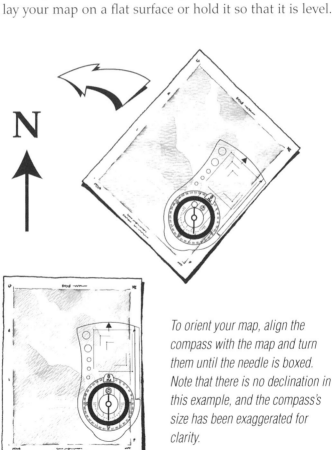

To orient your map, align the compass with the map and turn them until the needle is boxed. Note that there is no declination in this example, and the compass's size has been exaggerated for clarity.

Place your compass on the map so that the base plate runs along either the left or right margin and the direction-of-travel arrow is pointing toward north—the top of the map. Then box the needle by rotating the entire map without disturbing the compass base plate. Your map is now oriented to the surrounding landscape.

With some maps, you can also place your compass over the declination diagram and rotate the map until the needle is aligned with the magnetic north vector. This method can only be used of course on maps with a declination diagram. It won't work with maps that list declination but don't have a diagram, such as those you may find traveling outside of North America.

Bearings

Bearings are simply directions given in degrees between 0 and 360; you can think of them as more precise versions of the cardinal directions. To follow a bearing, first write it down on your map, just in case. Then turn the dial so that the bearing appears at the index line, and box the needle by holding the compass steady and turning your body. The direction-of-travel arrow should now be pointing along the bearing, toward your new objective. If you have a compass with a mirror and sight, now is the time to use it.

Pick out a distinct landmark (such as an unusually shaped boulder or a particularly tall tree) that lies directly along your bearing, between you and your objective. You then just walk directly to the landmark and repeat the process, choosing another landmark on the same bearing, until you arrive at your destination. Try to choose features that will be in sight until you reach them, but that are as far away as possible. The more intermediate landmarks you have to sight, the more you introduce opportunities for error.

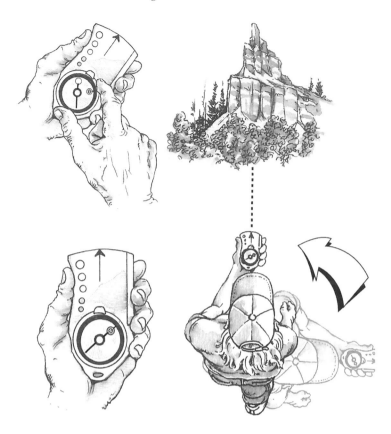

To follow a bearing, dial the bezel until the bearing appears at the index line, and turn your body to box the needle. You can then follow the bearing to your destination.

Going around large obstacles like a cliff or a lake on your bearing can be tricky. There are two ways to do it. The first is to sight beyond the obstacle. Say you have to go around a lake, for example. You would simply sight an intermediate on the other side of the lake, put the compass away, walk around the lake to your landmark, and start again. This is the fastest and most accurate method.

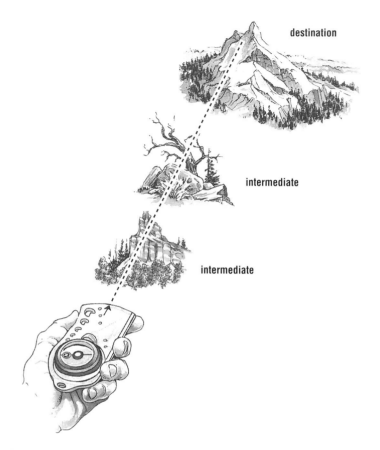

Use intermediate landmarks that lie along your bearing to help you keep moving in the right direction.

If you can't see a good intermediate past the obstacle, walk left or right, in a perpendicular line away from the bearing, until you can get by. Count the number of steps you take away from the bearing. Then walk forward, past the obstacle, following the direction-of-travel arrow so that you are walking parallel to the original bearing. When you've cleared the obstacle, count the same number of steps back to your bearing. While it may be

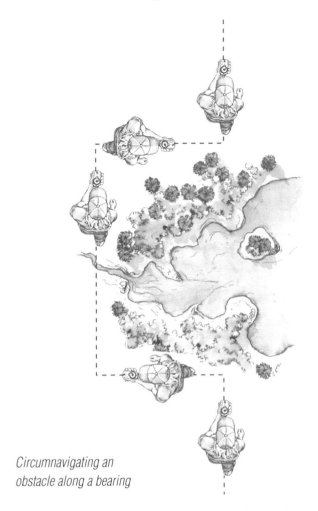

*Circumnavigating an
obstacle along a bearing*

your only option sometimes, this practice is time-consuming, prone to error, and best avoided if possible.

For those who work on search-and-rescue teams or compete in adventure races or other competitive navigation events, following a bearing quickly and accurately is the key to success. Practice sighting quickly and jogging from intermediate to intermediate without ever stopping completely. Try looking at your compass while you are moving. Brunton and Suunto also make orienteering thumb compasses that attach to your wrist and thumb to be read on the fly; if you need to move quickly, a thumb compass makes an excellent backup to your base-plate compass.

If you find yourself trying to follow a bearing in the dark or without adequate landmarks, you have at least two options. The

One technique for following a bearing in the dark is to have someone wear a headlamp and sight them as they walk forward. You can direct them left and right as needed.

first is to simply march along with your eyes on the compass, following the direction-of-travel arrow while keeping the needle boxed. The second, more accurate (but slower) method is to have a teammate walk ahead and take bearings on her. If it is dark, have her wear a second headlamp backward so that you can still see her. She should begin by walking about 50 feet or so out in front of you. As she moves forward, you should sight her every minute or so and give verbal directions ("Move right five steps," for example) to keep her on the bearing. The team should then walk toward her, repeating the process until the destination is reached.

TAKING A BEARING FROM THE TERRAIN

There are many reasons you may need to take a bearing from the terrain. Imagine that you can see your objective, a distant peak. However, a heavily forested valley lies between you and the peak. You realize that, as you descend into the valley, you will lose sight of the peak and could get off route. By taking a bearing on the peak before descending, you set your compass to guide you through the valley in a straight line toward the peak. You can now follow the bearing until you emerge from the trees and can see the land features again.

To take a bearing from the terrain, hold your compass at chest level directly in front of you, pointing the direction-of-travel arrow at your objective. Then, while holding the base plate level, rotate the bezel to box the needle. Your bearing is the number on the azimuth ring at the index line.

If your compass has a sighting mirror, you can precisely sight your objective at eye level using the gunsight notch on the top of the mirror. First adjust the mirror so that you can see the bezel well enough to box the needle while the base plate is level. The gunsight, the center line dividing the mirror, and the peep sight (at the bottom of the mirror on some models) all need to be lined up on your objective. As you take the bearing,

Taking a bearing on a terrain feature: with your direction-of-travel arrow pointing at the landmark, turn the bezel so the needle is boxed.

imagine a laser beam coming out from between your eyes, through the compass sights all the way to your destination.

TAKING A BEARING FROM A MAP

Sometimes, you can't see your objective to take a bearing on it. What would you do if, in the previous example, it got dark once you were already down in the forested valley? What if you had forgotten to take a terrain bearing before it got dark or a storm blew in? In situations like this, if you have been keeping track of where you are on the map, hope is not lost—you can get your bearing from the map. All you need to know is where your current location and your objective are on the map.

There are several ways to take a bearing from the map, but the simplest is as follows: After orienting the map with your compass, line up the base plate along the imaginary line between your location and your objective, with the direction-of-travel arrow pointed toward your objective. For more precision, draw in this line on the map. While holding the base plate on the line,

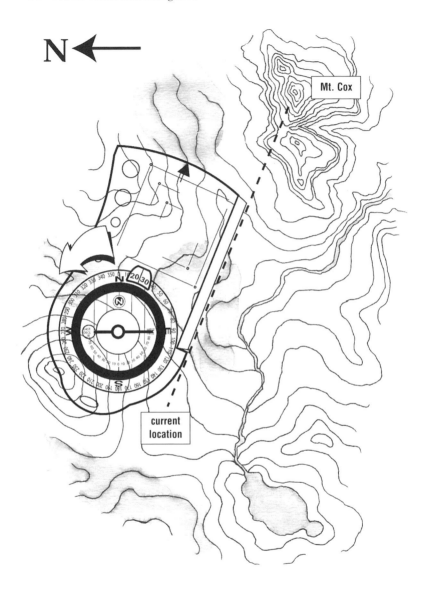

Taking a bearing from a map: once the needle has been boxed, the bearing will be at the index line.

turn the dial until the needle is boxed. Then simply read your bearing at the index line and follow it.

Other methods of taking bearings involve adding or subtracting declination. For many navigators, these can lead to error and thus are not covered in this book. Doing math in your head can get you into trouble, especially when you're tired. Occasionally, navigation geeks will argue about which method is best. You may hear folks talk about "true" versus "magnetic" bearings. If someone in your hiking group brings this up, don't let them confuse you. Politely tell them to lead, follow, or get out of the way.

If you are already accustomed to taking a bearing using grid lines on a map, continue to do what works for you. Done correctly, either method will get you where you need to go. What is important is to find what works best for you and be consistent to reduce the likelihood of mistakes.

BACK BEARINGS

If you have to go a particularly long distance on a bearing, consider using a back bearing to make sure you stay on track. This is a quick and simple procedure. Before you start to follow your original bearing, turn around so that you are facing directly away from your objective. You can tell you are facing the right way when you have boxed the south-seeking end of the needle. Be sure to rotate your body and the compass—don't touch that dial. While facing in this direction, find a large, distinct landmark that lies directly in front of you.

Then turn around and begin hiking toward your objective. Stop occasionally to turn around and box the south-seeking end of the needle. The direction-of-travel arrow should be pointing directly toward your starting point, the landmark beyond it, and any other intermediate landmarks you've passed so far. If these elements are not aligned, you have strayed from the bearing.

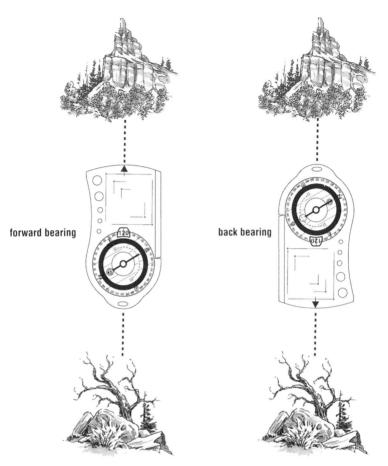

forward bearing   back bearing

Taking back bearings helps you to stay on route when following a long bearing.

PLOTTING A BEARING ONTO A MAP

By reversing the process for taking a bearing from a map, you can plot a bearing onto a map. This skill is useful for locating yourself or identifying a distant land feature on the map. If you keep up with your current location on the map (like a good navigator), you will rarely need to plot a bearing to locate yourself. Nonetheless, it can take some people years to develop an eye for distinguishing similar land features that lie in the same general direction. When time is not an issue, being able to plot bearings well can help with this.

Let's say you know your current location on the map, but are having trouble distinguishing between several peaks to the northeast. After orienting your map and marking your current location on it, take a field bearing on the landmark you wish to locate. Once you've established the bearing, don't even think of touching that dial. Next, place a bottom corner of the base plate on your current location, so that the direction-of-travel arrow is generally pointing away from it and toward your objective. Hold the corner there while rotating the base plate until the needle is boxed. Then draw a line from your location along the edge of the compass and across the map. If your compass has a mirror, open it to give the compass a longer edge. If you still need to extend the line past the compass and didn't bring a ruler, you

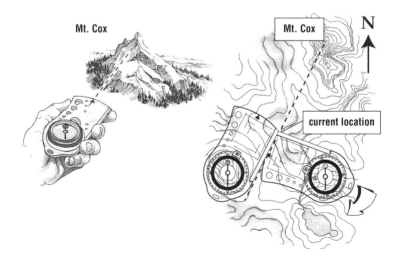

Transferring a bearing onto a map: take a bearing on a landmark, place a corner of the compass on your destination, and rotate it until the needle is boxed.

can do some creative map folding and use the map itself as a straightedge. In any case, provided the line is long enough, the landmark in question will lie somewhere along it.

LOCATING YOUR POSITION USING BEARINGS

There are at least two ways to locate yourself with bearings: using line position and triangulating.

If you are lucky enough to be traveling along a defined linear feature that is generally straight for a mile or so, such as a ridge, trail, or drainage, you can locate yourself by plotting a single bearing on your map. You simply trace a line along the land feature you are following, orient your map, and plot a bearing onto your map from a visible, known landmark, preferably

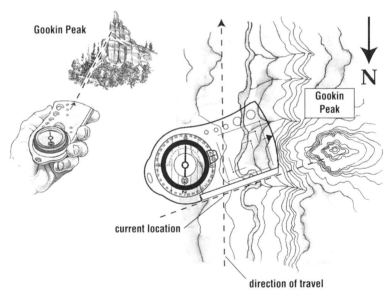

If you are following a trail or another relatively straight feature, you can find your approximate location by taking a bearing on a nearby landmark. Here, the navigator uses a creek and nearby butte to determine her location.

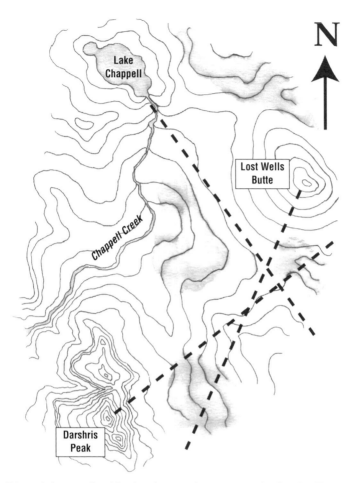

Triangulation entails taking bearings on three separate landmarks. The triangle they form contains your location.

one at about 90 degrees to the linear feature. Your location is near the point at which the two lines intersect.

But what if you have lost your position and are not on a linear feature? If you can positively identify three or more visible land features, you can plot bearings to them to find yourself with great accuracy. This self-locating method is known as triangulation. Your accuracy will be the best if the landmarks are spaced evenly around you—more than 60 degrees is ideal. After orienting your map, you take field bearings on each landmark, like you did for the linear feature method. Draw straight lines along the compass edge for each bearing, extending it on either side of the landmark. These three lines should form a triangle, inside of which is your location. The more accurate your bearings are, the smaller the triangle will be.

If you can identify only two landmarks, you can still plot bearings to give a less precise location. The process is similar to triangulation, except you are left with the intersection of two bearings instead of a triangle. Your location is somewhere near this intersection.

If you find yourself triangulating often, you probably need to work on your terrain association and pay better attention to your location as you travel. Think of triangulation as more of a last resort than a routinely used skill.

Exercise 1: Taking and Following a Bearing on a Landmark

Start in a familiar location, whether urban or rural. Take a moment to orient yourself, finding your local declination and setting it on your compass. Which way is true north? Is it where you expected it to be? Take a moment to let your mind associate what your compass is telling you with the land around you.

Take a bearing from where you are now on a water tower, tall hill, or other large visible landmark, the farther away the better. Then use your compass alone to follow the bearing toward the landmark. (If you are in an urban setting, be mindful of traffic.) If there are parked cars, buildings, rivers, or other obstacles blocking your path, use the techniques described on pages

48–50 to get back on your bearing. Stop every 100 meters or so and take a back bearing. Are you still on track?

Repeat this process three more times, sighting landmarks and following bearings in each cardinal direction.

Exercise 2: Off-Trail Loop Hike on Bearings

This exercise could take three to eight hours depending on the distance and terrain you select. It requires fifteen to twenty minutes of map work before hiking. If you have friends joining you on the hike, you may want to do part A at home in advance.

If you are hopelessly city-locked and have a map of the right scale, you can practice the skills in exercise 2 (as well as exercise 3) in an urban setting, taking bearings on buildings and so forth. However, just as immersion is the best way to learn a foreign language, nothing will improve your ability to navigate in the wilderness like navigating in the wilderness. If it is difficult for you to travel to a park or other undeveloped lands suitable for practicing compass use, you might choose to take a trip and do everything in one adventurous day.

Before heading into the field, make sure you have gained some map-reading experience on trail and are comfortable with your survival skills in case you become lost or injured. We strongly recommend taking a friend or two, particularly if you are new to the backcountry. Don't forget to leave a travel plan and pack a lunch and the essential gear listed on page xii.

PART A: PLANNING THE ROUTE

Begin by setting the correct declination, orienting your map, and marking the location of your starting point (often called the trailhead on your way in to the wilderness and the roadhead on your way out). Then pick at least three recognizable landmarks to which you could hike. Your goal is to plan a loop hike that will visit all three landmarks. We'll call these landmarks your "waypoints." They can be ponds, small hills, drainage confluences, trail intersections, or even railroad or power line crossings. They should be at least a mile apart and visible from a short distance. Try to choose waypoints that will be visible from one another—two hilltops, for example.

Mark the waypoints clearly on the map and number them from 1 to 3.

The next step is to pencil in your route on the map. Chapter 3 covers route planning in depth, but for now your main concerns should be to make things as simple as possible. As you plan your route, measure the total distance and elevation gain. Is the distance realistic for your party? Write down your estimated return time in the margin of the map—remember, off-trail travel is slower. If your route is too long, too full of obstacles, or likely to leave you out after dark, it is probably too complicated for this exercise. Go elsewhere and find new waypoints.

If the route is manageable, write down your estimated times of arrival (ETAs) next to each waypoint. Plot bearings on the map from point to point in the order you wish to follow them, making sure the direction-of-travel arrow is pointed in the direction you will be traveling each time. Write the bearing beside each line you've drawn to remind you where to set your bezel at each waypoint. Double-check that the bearings you've plotted do not go over any cliffs or large bodies of water that you can't circumnavigate.

PART B: FOLLOWING THE ROUTE

When you've become a more experienced navigator, you will be able to decide whether to follow a bearing or just use your map based on your judgment of the terrain, visibility, and so on. For the purposes of this exercise, try to follow your route from point to point, using your map as little as possible. Focus instead on routefinding and staying on each compass bearing.

If you need to sight intermediate landmarks as you follow the bearings, do so at the greatest distance possible for increased accuracy. Also sight each waypoint from time to time as you approach it. Is it on the same bearing you are following?

If you start out on a bearing and seem to be going the wrong direction, stop and reorient your map to check that you haven't plotted it incorrectly. Because you have your bearings written down, you can readjust your bezel to orient the map whenever necessary. Just be sure to reset the bearing when you are finished.

Keep track of your pace. Are you meeting your ETAs? Have you passed your waypoint? Is there a visible feature that will tell you if you've gone too far?

When you've successfully traveled from your third waypoint to your starting point, congratulate yourself—you've just planned and followed your own off-trail route! What worked well? Where did you run into trouble? If you struggled with the exercise, consider practicing plotting bearings at home and then trying it again in another area.

Exercise 3: Using Bearings to Locate Your Position

This exercise should take from a couple of hours to a full day, depending on the location you choose to do your triangulating. The key to success in this exercise is planning well in advance and choosing a good spot with lots of recognizable landmarks. The more land features there are, the better. (If you can't visit an area with enough topographic relief to sight landmarks from a distance, don't drive yourself crazy trying to take bearings on landmarks you can't identify. Save this exercise for a trip to the mountains or canyons.)

Spend some time looking at maps in advance, and ask others for advice if you aren't sure where to go. Most outdoor retailers can recommend good day hikes in their area. You will also need fairly good weather in order to see distant landmarks. Plan to go early on a day without precipitation or fog. Once again, consider bringing one or more friends and doing your route planning in advance.

PART A: PLANNING THE ROUTE

Choose an area with distinct land features that you will be able to pick out on the map and identify easily on land. Remember, if you can't positively identify at least two landmarks, you can't use bearings to find your location. An ideal spot for this exercise would be an open valley with high ridges on both sides.

In addition to your starting point, mark a small triangle on your map in the place where you plan to do your triangulation. We'll call this your turnaround point. Pencil in the route from your roadhead to the turnaround point. It would be best if your route follows a trail or drainage, so that a) it will be quicker and easier to follow, and b) you will have a linear reference point, and can determine your location from a single bearing.

PART B: FOLLOWING THE ROUTE

As you hike toward the turnaround point, identify up to five land features that you can positively locate on the map. Try to use features at different distances and directions from the route you are following.

Each time you can sight another feature, stop and try to identify your exact location using terrain association. Then, double-check your accuracy by locating your position with bearings. How did you do? Were you close without using the compass?

Once you arrive at your turnaround point, you are ready to practice triangulation as described in this chapter. Can you positively identify the land features you were expecting to see just looking at the map? Mark your location first using terrain association only. Now, go ahead and triangulate. How large is the triangle created by your bearings? Is it close to the position you estimated without using the compass?

On the hike back, stop in different places and take bearings on some of the features you sighted on your way in.

Conclusion

If you've spent some time out doing these exercises, you are well on your way to competence with your compass skills. Keep things in perspective, however. Think of the compass as an essential piece of equipment in your navigation toolbox, but one that ranks third behind your brain and a good map.

PLANNING AND
FOLLOWING A ROUTE

In wilderness navigation, good routefinding means planning and following an efficient route—one that balances speed, safety, and energy conservation. It also means anticipating and minimizing your group's exposure to hazards, recognizing them on the map as you plan your route and on the ground as you travel. The difficulty of the route must match the abilities of the party.

In 2002, I was leading a team in the Eco-Challenge expedition race. On the second day, I took the team up and over a very steep ridge to shave about 10 miles off a 40-mile trek through dense Fijian rainforest. As is often the case, there was no way to tell from the maps where the forest density changed. After six hours of steep bushwhacking through the most brutal vines and bamboo we had ever seen, we reached the top of the narrow ridge. A series of short vertical drops over a mile-long, 60-degree slope covered in loose rock and vegetation lay ahead. We were out of water and needed to get to the river at the bottom quickly, so we headed down. As we slid, fell, and climbed our way down the slope, vines and small trees pulled loose. Cliffs forced us to reroute five times. At different points, two of my teammates fell 20 to 30 feet; had they not been wearing helmets, they could have been critically injured. By the time we made it to the river, we had dropped from fifteenth to fortieth place. The other teams, who had followed the river the entire way, had to cover more ground but were able to do so at a steady pace with few routefinding challenges. Not only were they ahead, they hadn't taken unnecessary risks and wasted valuable energy.

The navigation mistakes I made in Fiji are common when planning and following an off-trail route. Here they are one by one:

1. The route was not appropriate for the entire team. I was the only rock climber on the team and I chose a route that was too steep and did not take into account my teammates' experience and desires. The small-scale (1:100,000) maps we had were not detailed enough to show short cliffs. I should have erred on the side of caution.

2. There were no easily identifiable handrails (see page 76) for long sections of the route, forcing us to travel by compass bearings alone in dense jungle for many hours.

3. There were no water sources on the route I chose.

4. We were too inexperienced with that environment (Fijian jungle) to accurately predict how dense the brush was and how slow the bushwhacking might be. Consequently, my time estimates were wrong.

5. When it started to get rough, we kept pushing on instead of accepting our mistake and turning back for the longer but easier route.

I knew not to do these things and had even taught others not to do them. How is it that we can make the same navigational mistakes again and again? It's similar to the way people become addicted to gambling. "What if it really pays off this time?" you say to yourself. The temptation to find that secret shortcut and be the navigation hero is very strong. If you are leading others, however, you owe it to them to ask yourself what is really motivating you to choose the routes you do. What are the risks and potential consequences? Consult the others in your group. Make conservative decisions when potential losses are significant.

If it starts looking too challenging, stop and be realistic about turning back. There is no such thing as "lost time." Every time you double back, you are learning a valuable lesson. Be willing to accept that you may not have chosen the best route for that group on that day. If you are going to end up turning back, it's best to make that decision as soon as possible. Mistakes are part of navigation. Forget the blame and shame—just turn around and get going in the right direction. Others in your group may complain about turning back, but those complaints are nothing compared to unplanned nights out, hospital bills, or worse.

Understanding Your Public Lands

Whether you live in the United States, Canada, or elsewhere, having a basic understanding of public lands in your country will allow you to plan your travels more easily and efficiently. About 32 percent of the land in the United States is managed by federal agencies—that's 727 million acres. Knowing who manages the land you are planning to visit will allow you to get better information on the area and may prevent you from accidentally breaking the law.

In the United States, there are four major land management agencies: the National Park Service, the Bureau of Land Management, the Fish and Wildlife Service, and the Forest Service.

The *National Park Service* (NPS) was founded in 1916 to preserve the nation's "crown jewels." It is part of the Department of the Interior, and its stated goal is to protect resources and provide for public enjoyment. Some of the more famous lands managed by the NPS include Yosemite National Park in California, Denali National Park in Alaska, and Grand Canyon National Park in Arizona.

The *Bureau of Land Management* (BLM) was created in 1949, initially to manage lands that had few trees and were seen to have limited value. Today, the BLM's mandate is for multiple use, which includes all forms of outdoor recreation, grazing, timber harvesting, watershed maintenance, fish and wildlife management, mining, and cultural resource preservation. The BLM oversees the nation's largest federal land mass, more than 270 million acres.

The *US Fish and Wildlife Service* (USFWS) was founded as part of the Department of Interior in 1956. Its goal is to protect fish and wildlife and their habitats. The USFWS also maintains lists of threatened and endangered species.

The *US Forest Service* (USFS), created in 1905, is part of the Department of Agriculture. It manages the nation's supply of timber. Today, its goal is multiple use for the country's forests—both harvesting and recreation.

In 1964, Congress passed the Wilderness Act, which designates certain areas of public lands federally protected wilderness areas. There are 95.6 million acres of protected wilderness in the United States. Wilderness areas are managed by the agencies above; they do not allow roads, motorized equipment (such as off-road vehicles and chainsaws), mechanized equipment (such as bicycles), permanent structures, mining, or timber harvesting. Additionally, there are Wilderness Study Areas (WSAs) deemed to have wilderness qualities, which are currently being studied for possible wilderness designation. You should always be aware of whether or not you are traveling in a wilderness area so that you can abide by the federal laws of that area.

In addition to federal lands, states, provinces, and cities also manage parks that may be suitable for backcountry navigation. Get to know what public lands are available in your area. In a few states, there is more state than federal land to visit.

In states like Texas, where there is much more private than public land, you may be tempted to plan a route that crosses a short section of private land. Unfortunately, a short stretch of private land often separates two much larger areas of public land. When you are planning a long route, it can seem easy to just sneak across that sliver and continue your route. *Resist the temptation to trespass.* The sorts of people who own large sections of land adjoining public lands tend to value their land rights, independence, and privacy rather highly. They also often own guns and know how to use them. Chances are good that you won't be the first person to take a shortcut across their property. Aside from breaking trespassing laws, you might actually be endangering your life, particularly in the western United States and other areas where poaching is a problem. If you are traveling to foreign countries, you should be even more diligent about making sure that you are on public lands. Check before leaving home and double-check with locals when you arrive at your destination to make sure that you are permitted to be where you are planning to go.

You can download a map showing all of the public lands of the United States at http://nationalatlas.gov/printable.html# fedlands. Contact information for relevant land management agencies can be found on page 183.

Choosing a Route

After you've determined your objective, start designing your route by looking at maps to determine where you have vehicle access to start and end the route. Are you leaving a vehicle somewhere and returning to that same spot? Can someone drop you off or pick you up? Will you need to leave a car at another trailhead?

If your route will include off-trail travel, keep in mind the price that you will pay in time and energy. In about 90 percent of the areas you will visit, traveling off-trail will take longer and tire you out more quickly than hiking on a trail. (The other 10 percent are open meadows, deserts, snow-covered areas, ice, large rock slabs, or any open areas where the surface is not much different than that of a trail.) Off-trail often means you have to deal with hazards that a trail might avoid, such as exposure to lightning, steep snow or ice, rocks and boulders, downed trees, fast-moving water, and dense vegetation. As you plan an off-trail route, you should build in plenty of extra time to recover from errors.

Being able to judge when and when not to head away from the trail is the mark of a good navigator. Some of the most beautiful wilderness areas in the world do not have trails. There will certainly be times when it is to your advantage to travel off-trail to shorten the distance to your objective. Make sure you know what you're doing, though—this is how I got into trouble in Fiji.

If you'll be going through mountainous areas, remember that more trees usually means a more stable slope. In North America, north-facing slopes tend to be more thickly vegetated and will have snow longer than other aspects, which is good for skiing and ice climbing but bad for hiking and biking. In any given mountain range, the snowline, treeline, and tundra zones should appear at about the same elevation throughout.

If your trip will take more than a day, you'll need to plan where to camp along the route. Your first thought in choosing campsites should be safety. Is the campsite too close to a steep slope that could avalanche or release falling rocks? Are there any dead trees that could fall on your tent if the wind picks up? Upstream weather can cause unexpected rises in river levels and flooding in canyon country—is the area you are in subject to flash flooding? Is it too exposed to the wind and weather? What is a reasonable distance for this group to hike today? Consider planning alternate campsites that are easier to reach in case you can't make it to your primary campsite.

If you want to avoid crowds, seek advice from land managers about less-visited areas and quieter times to visit. Choose a durable surface to camp, such as pine duff, sand, snow, a rocky slab, or any nonvegetated area. With the proper equipment, you can camp comfortably on almost any flat surface. Plan your campsites so that they are at least 200 feet from water. This will decrease the impact on overused areas and leave the water accessible to wildlife. In many areas of the United States, it is illegal to camp closer than 200 feet.

Even if you're not planning to camp, your hiking group should be self-sufficient and have all the necessary gear to survive overnight. This allows folks to relax when navigating, knowing that if they can't find the way this evening, they can camp and look again in the morning.

On-Trail Travel

All trails are not created equal. They can vary dramatically depending on the terrain, the season, who built them, how they are maintained, and for whom they were originally designed. Some may have mile markers and signs at every intersection, while others may be completely unmarked except at the trailhead.

Trails can be marked in several different ways. Some trails are indicated by blazes—slash marks made in trees with an ax or machete at about four to six feet from the ground. The phrase "blazing trails" comes from pioneers who originally marked trees to establish trails through western forests. In National Forests in the United States, trees are usually blazed with a short slash mark below a longer slash mark, like an upside-down letter "i." On well-blazed trails, each blaze is visible from the one before it. Trees are often blazed on both sides so that they can be recognized from either direction. In the forested areas where

Common trail markers

blazes are used, however, there are often animals (bears and elk, for example) that commonly rub or scratch trees, which removes the bark from them. A little time in the field will make it easier for you to recognize the difference between a long, symmetrical blaze and an animal sign.

In order to better preserve trailside trees, some land managers are now using metallic tags to mark a trail rather than blazes. Others will paint a blaze on the tree rather than cutting into the bark.

Another way to tell if you're on trail in a forest is by looking for log cuts. Those who build and maintain trails have to cut fallen trees to clear a path. These cut trees sit on the sides of maintained trails and are easy to distinguish from trees that have fallen naturally.

In treeless areas, rock cairns are often built to keep folks on the trail. Cairns are rocks piled up between knee- and waist-high. Cairns are a simple way to stay on the trail, but they can become a visual nuisance in high-traffic areas. If you build one, be sure to dismantle it on your way out. Cairns are unnecessary in areas where the trail is easy to follow.

Have you ever been following a trail that seemed to disappear? There are several reasons that can happen. Animals routinely use human-made trails to move more easily from place to place in the wilderness. However, while we build in switchbacks and turns to prevent erosion and make the trail easier to hike or ride, animals are not that interested in switchbacks. It is not uncommon to see game trails that continue on where the human-made trail makes a sharp turn. If there is enough animal traffic and you are not anticipating a turn in the trail, it is easy for you to miss your turn and continue on a game trail that will eventually disappear. Be mindful of trails that make sudden direction changes. When the trail seems to narrow suddenly or the trail surface changes, stop and take a quick look around. Are you missing a turn? Did you just start heading up or down a hill? Is there a switchback covered in snow?

If you are trying to follow a trail but are not sure you are on it, stop and look back. Will you be able to find your way back to the trail? In hilly areas, it's easy to meander downhill and off the trail. If you were traversing along a hill when you lost the trail, chances are good that the trail is above you. People tend to take the path of least resistance and head downhill when they are feeling lost or having difficulty following a trail.

You should either be on the trail or off the trail. Never walk beside trails or cut switchbacks, which causes erosion.

Off-Trail Travel

Following an off-trail route is usually more challenging than just moving along a trail, but there are some techniques you can use to make your navigation easier. One example is taking advantage of long view corridors when traveling in heavily forested areas. A see, or shot, is the distance that is visible in a given

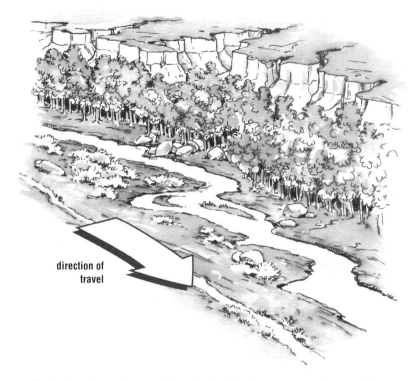

Handrails such as rivers or cliffs make it relatively easy to move in a straight line.

direction from where you are standing. If you are traveling off-trail in a forest or jungle, look for the longest see in the general direction you want to travel. As you continue, keep moving ahead along the best see which parallels your intended route. When you come to the end of a see, repeat the process until you reach your objective or reach a more open area. The first and second person should be communicating and making most of the route decisions in heavy brush. The idea is to keep the whole group moving in the right direction, even though some individuals may stop briefly.

The first things to look for when planning an off-trail route are handrails, also known as line features. A handrail is simply a linear land feature that parallels your route. You may walk right next to it, or it may be visible from a distance, but as you travel, you should be able to see it from time to time. If you can maintain a constant distance between you and a straight handrail, you will know you are traveling in a straight line. Cliffs, ridges, drainages, shorelines, fences, power lines, and train tracks all make good handrails. (You can handrail roads or trails, but why not just walk on them if you can see them?) While you are rarely able to follow the same handrail from your origin to your destination, there is often some feature that you can handrail for at least a leg of your journey.

One way to better reach an objective that lies on a linear feature, like a trail, is by intentionally aiming off from your objective. Say you are traveling off-trail and you need to locate a trail intersection. If you head directly for it, unless your navigation is perfect, chances are good that you will wind up intersecting the trail somewhere to the left or right of the intersection. Which way do you go? If you don't have great visibility, you now have only a 50 percent chance of heading the right way. By purposefully aiming off a few degrees from the proper bearing, you know what side of the objective you are on and which way you need to travel.

Another critical tool for navigating off-trail is using what are known as catching features or backstops. Any feature that lies beyond your objective and is more or less perpendicular to your route can be a backstop. It simply needs to be something that you can recognize so that you will know when you've gone too far and passed your objective. A river, lake, fence line, mountain, canyon, road, trail, or any other obvious large feature will work. If possible, you should always have a backstop in mind as you travel off-trail. Ask yourself, "How will I know if I overshoot my objective?"

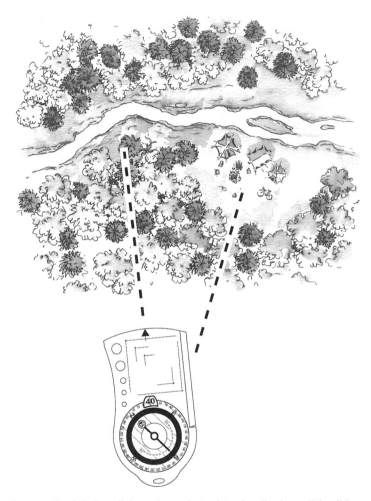

An example of aiming off: here, the navigator intentionally aims a little off from her target so she can follow the river to camp.

Points along your route at which you leave a trail or handrail are called attack points. They should be easily recognizable; ask yourself, "How will I know when to leave the trail?" Good attack points include trail intersections and the places where a trail crosses a drainage or tree line.

direction
of travel

Use backstops to tell if you've gone too far.

Special Travel Situations

STEEP TERRAIN

Mountaineers use rating systems to describe how steep and difficult a route up a mountain may be. These systems provide a common language for climbers and hikers to discuss the difficulty of a route. North American climbers generally use the Yosemite Decimal System (YDS). In the YDS, there are five classes of terrain:

> **Class 1:** Simple walking. City sidewalks and most trails are class 1 terrain.

The Yosemite Decimal System

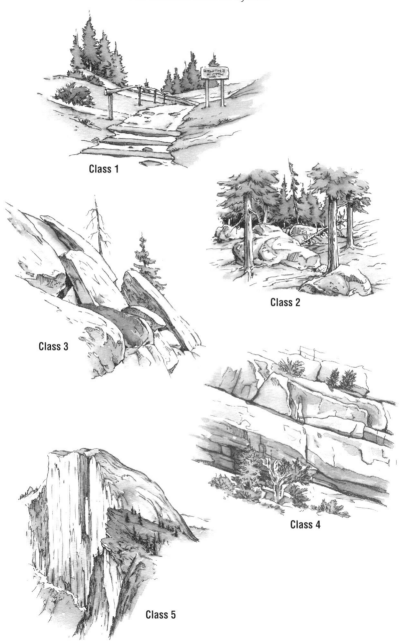

Class 1

Class 2

Class 3

Class 4

Class 5

Class 2: Steep hiking on-trail or off-trail. Most class 2 terrain is found in mountains or canyons.

Class 3: Scrambling. You may need to use your hands occasionally. Steep boulder fields are an example of class 3 terrain. There is the potential for short falls. Some people may carry a rope just in case.

Class 4: Simple climbing where falls can be fatal but are unlikely. Many will choose to use ropes in class 4 terrain.

Class 5: Rock climbing. Climbing class 5 terrain should involve the use of a rope, belaying, and other specific climbing techniques. Climbers subdivide this class into difficulty ratings from 5.0 to 5.15.

Unless you are properly trained and are planning to go rock climbing, class 4 and class 5 terrain should be avoided. During our misadventure in Fiji, we were descending unroped in class 4 terrain—a potentially critical mistake. Class 3 terrain is rather slow going and is also best avoided in most cases.

There are certainly times when the temptation to shorten the route by traveling through steeper terrain will be great. Occasionally, it really is faster to go up and over that steep ridge than to walk all the way around it. Before heading up into steep terrain, ask yourself these questions:

- What are the risks and hazards of going up and over? What is the weather doing? Will we have enough water? Is there danger of rockfall?
- What is the energy cost of going over the hill? Will we still have the time and energy to make it all the way to our objective today?
- Could it actually be slower for this group going over the top?
- Will the routefinding be harder or easier?

BOULDERS, TALUS, SCREE, AND TILL

As a mountain erodes with age, fields of broken-down rocks form on its sides. Those who travel often in the mountains divide these rock fields into separate categories depending on the size of the individual rock chunks.

The largest chunks are boulders, which can range in size anywhere from the size of an average ice chest (the kind you might use to keep drinks cold at the beach) to a very large house. Boulder fields are tedious and dangerous. Traveling through large boulders is slow and requires good balance and occasionally some rudimentary rock-climbing skills. Avoid these when you can.

Talus ranges in size from a small ice chest down to the size of a softball. While traveling on talus is not pleasant, it is usually not as time-consuming and energy-draining as boulders. When talus is on a very steep slope, however, there is the danger of someone above knocking a rock down on those below. It's also nice to have shoes or boots that protect your ankles from loose rocks when traveling on talus.

Scree includes any rock smaller than a softball but larger than a grain of sand. Scree fields can make a fantastic descent route if you have gaiters to keep the pebbles from getting into your boots. In New Zealand, I once "boot-skied" a scree field that was two kilometers long and was able to descend 2,000 feet in a few minutes. Going UP a scree field is an entirely different story. Depending on the shape of the scree, you may create a small avalanche with each step you take. At times, ascending a scree slope feels like taking two steps back for every one step forward. Even doing an ascending traverse can be slow going on scree.

In mountainous areas carved by glaciers, you may come across glacial till. Till consists of tiny bits of rock, the size of sand grains or smaller, that have been ground up by glaciers. Walking on till is like walking on a beach that has been tilted up and dropped on the side of a mountain. It can be slow going, but generally not as slow to ascend as scree or boulders.

THICK VEGETATION

The most efficient routes usually stick to open terrain. The advantage of open terrain is not just that it's easier to walk on, but also that it lets you see greater distances and make navigational decisions earlier.

Typically, ridges are less vegetated and offer better visibility than drainages. Drainages are often choked with vegetation that thrives on the water available there. Some of the nastier varieties of trees and shrubbery to travel through are: thick bamboo in jungles, alders on steep slopes in western North America, marsh willows in the Rockies, countless thorny vines in the tropics, and manzanita and cat's claw in the southwestern United States. Cacti can be rough in the desert Southwest but are more easily avoided. As you develop an eye for travel in the area you are visiting, you will know what kinds of brush to avoid.

DESERTS, ICE FIELDS, AND OTHER WIDE-OPEN SPACES

Navigating in featureless terrain is all about maintaining your heading and keeping track of the distance you are covering. There may not be a trail for many miles. While it is possible to navigate with just the sun and stars, you can almost eliminate the guesswork by using a compass and/or GPS to maintain your heading.

Today, most folks who travel across open spaces for extended periods will use a handheld GPS to give them their location, pace, and distance to destination. However, if you are using a map and compass, take the time to determine exactly what bearing you will follow across the flats to your next recognizable land feature. In some areas, you could travel for days on one bearing. Carefully keeping track of your pace and distance traveled will relieve any anxiety, particularly if you are on a tight schedule.

TRAVELING AT NIGHT

If you will be traveling much in the wilderness, it's a good idea to have some experience traveling at night. In an emergency, you'll have a much better understanding of the possibilities and limitations of nighttime travel. Also, it can be a lot of fun!

There are a number of extra risks to consider before traveling in the backcountry at night. Not only is it hard to see land features to orient yourself, it is often hard to see where you are stepping or even read the map. The potential for accidental falls, surprise animal encounters, and becoming woefully lost increases dramatically. Your body will be telling you it's time for bed. You will also move considerably slower at night and your pace may shorten slightly.

In the steep terrain of the canyons or mountains, the potential for walking directly off a small cliff is certainly real. The faster you are moving, the greater the hazard.

If you combine all of the above with sleep deprivation, you are in for quite a challenge. Plan your night navigation very carefully, or expect reluctant sleep in an unplanned spot.

When planning a nighttime route, choose the path which will be easiest to follow even if it is a bit longer. Handrails, backstops, and compass readings become critical. Changes in the slope angle you are walking on may be the only indication of a hill you would have seen clearly from a distance in the daylight. You may need to count your paces (see page 85), particularly for off-trail travel.

While you might use Polaris to roughly orient your map, don't take compass bearings on stars, which are too imprecise.

The bearing on a star can be the same even between points miles apart.

Keeping the above in mind, plan a short on-trail route in an area that you are familiar with the first time you go out hiking at night. A nearby city or state park (one where crime is not a major concern) will work. Make it an adventure and take a few friends with you the first few times you go. Stick together. Don't consider longer distances or unfamiliar areas until you get comfortable with moving in the forest at night. When you do move on to traveling in unfamiliar backcountry areas at night, be sure to write a travel plan and bring essential gear.

Other Tips for Following Routes

PACE SETTING

The pace you set for your group will depend entirely on what your group goals for the day are. Are you out to snap some photos, enjoy the scenery, and have a picnic in a remote place? Or do you have to reach a specific campsite by nightfall? Do you have the entire day to cover several miles of easy hiking? Or are you in the middle of an adventure race? Everyone in the group should agree in advance what the goal for the day is and set a pace that suits the goal. If you are out to enjoy the scenery, rushing along with your eyes on your compass is not going to achieve your goal. Unless you really are in a race, don't stress everyone else out by acting like it. There are times to relax and take it easy and times to get moving.

For those times when you do need to move in a hurry, pay careful attention to stopping for breaks. Determine how many breaks you really need. More than one every hour may be excessive. Can you eat and drink while you are moving? When you stop, make sure someone keeps an eye on the time. A lot can be accomplished in a ten-minute break: you can change layers, refill water, grab some food, and tape that "hot spot" on your heel. Make sure that items you will need on the trail are accessible and not buried deep in your pack.

The person out front should be setting a pace that is sustainable for the whole group, given the terrain and length of time you will be traveling. As a pace-setter, it is your job to check in with other members of the group and make sure the pace is working for everyone. If someone is struggling to keep up, don't let him or her drift to the back. Put slower hikers in the middle or front so that the group can adjust to a pace that is manageable for everyone.

PACE COUNTING

Estimating your speed and then keeping an eye on your watch is by far the easiest way to gauge distance; it is also the least precise. Over longer distances and in times when precision is less important, use your hiking speed to estimate distance. To be accurate, you will need to know your speed with and without a pack, on and off the trail, in brush and in the open.

A more precise way to measure distance is pace counting. During an eight-mile hiking day, pace-counting the whole distance is simply impractical. But if you become interested in orienteering (see chapter 9), you will need to count paces at times.

Figuring out the length of your average pace is simple: see exercise 3 on page 88. Once you know your average length, you simply need to keep track of your paces. There are a number of ways to do this. Some people use beads on a string or pebbles moved from one hand to another or dropped in a pocket every one hundred paces. Find a system that works for you and apply it consistently as you travel.

CONTOURING

Losing elevation only to regain it later can be a frustrating drain on your group's energy. Two techniques that can be helpful in dealing with this are contouring and sidehilling. Contouring is maintaining the same elevation as you travel, as if you were walking along a contour line on a map. Often, steep terrain can be avoided this way.

Sidehilling is contouring off-trail on a steep slope. When you are sidehilling, each step with your uphill leg will be shorter than each step with your downhill leg. This means that your uphill leg is supporting your entire weight most of the time. If the hill is not very steep or the distance is not great, sidehilling is not a problem. If you are sidehilling in steep terrain for more than a quarter mile, your uphill leg muscles may begin to complain. Extended sidehilling is to be avoided. It is often easier to do an ascending traverse to the ridge above or descend to the base and parallel the hill.

CHECKING THE MAP

Your speed, experience, and memory will all play in to how often you should be looking at your map. Unless you are racing, you have nothing to lose by taking the time to stop and make sure you are on the right track. While you are practicing the exercises in this book, you should be looking at your map at least every five minutes unless you are cruising alongside a major river or trail with no junctions. Many navigators will study their map in detail the night before a long or tricky route to try and memorize as much of the route as they can. This allows them to spend less time looking at the map while they are moving. If visibility becomes a problem (nightfall, bad weather, etc.), you should be checking your map even more than usual.

You should orient your map every time you stop to look at it. Some navigators even keep their map oriented by turning it in their hands as they change directions. At the very least, try to keep your thumb on your location on the map as you travel. By using this technique, known as thumbing, you always know your approximate location on the map and don't have to relocate yourself each time you do a map check. You are also more likely to catch a wrong turn before you get disoriented.

STAYING FLEXIBLE

Be flexible. Your maps can only tell you so much. You may have to adjust your plans according to the weather and new information that you discover on the ground. Visualize your route in stages.

Be willing to stop and scout before moving ahead if you are unsure where to go. Seek higher ground for a better view if you need to. Scout in pairs with maps, then regroup to share the scouts' findings.

Exercise 1: Getting Off-Trail

Plan and follow your own off-trail route. Begin by taking some time to study the map and visualizing what the terrain will look like. What are the contour lines telling you about the shape of the terrain? Where are the hills and valleys? How far apart are they? Where will your field of view be blocked by hills in the foreground?

Then plan your route. Where will your attack point be? Are there any handrails or backstops you can use? Will the route be out and back, a loop, or a "lollipop" shape?

When you arrive at the trailhead, think of how well what you are seeing matches what you visualized. Does it look the way you expected it to?

Exercise 2: Staying Oriented

Plan another short hike (two to five miles) that travels mostly off-trail and forms a circle or loop. Keep your map out the whole time you are hiking, with your thumb on your location. Try to keep the map oriented so that north on the map is always pointing toward true north. Can you do it without looking at your compass?

Exercise 3: Learning Your Average Speed

There are two methods you can use to determine your average speed. The first is to measure your speed in various settings. Take a few minutes to study the chart of average mile times below.

AVERAGE SPEED CHART

Times in minutes per mile for an average person with no pack weight.

			Off-Trail	
	Road	Trail	Open Woods	Thick Brush
Walking				
Uphill	18	20	22	25+
Flat	15	16	18	20+
Running				
Uphill	11	12	13	N/A
Flat	9	10	11	N/A

Measure your personal average times along different stretches of some routes and fill in the chart. Obviously, how steep the terrain is will affect your time. The times above are for a slope between 5 and 10 degrees. If you are in a flatter area, take your time on a hill a quarter- or half-mile long and multiply. Be honest with yourself about your average times, as they will be used to help you estimate your speed in different situations. Take note of the conditions for each speed that you measure. What are your average times at night? How about with a heavy backpack?

AVERAGE SPEED CHART				

Times in minutes per mile for an average person with no pack weight.

			Off-Trail	
	Road	**Trail**	**Open Woods**	**Thick Brush**
Walking				
Uphill				
Flat				
Running				
Uphill				
Flat				

You also have the option of setting up a pace meter. Go to a track at a local school with a quarter-mile lap. Walk the distance with your pack on, counting every time your right foot hits the ground—it takes two steps to make one pace. How many paces does it take you to get around the track? Multiply that number by 4 to get a rough idea of how many paces it takes you to walk a mile. Divide 5,280 by *that* number to get your average pace length in feet. You can use a similar method on a football or soccer field. Count the number of paces it takes you to walk the field, and divide that number by 100 to get the length of your pace in yards (American football field) or meters (soccer field). Use the following values to convert between metric and English measurements:

1 kilometer = 1,000 meters = 3,281 feet = 1,094 yards
1 mile = 5,280 feet = 1,760 yards = 1,609 meters = 1.609
    kilometers

How do you think your pace length will change at night? How about going up or down a steep hill? Put your predictions to the test in the field and record the results for future route-planning.

CHAPTER 4 | ALTIMETERS

What Is an Altimeter (and Do I Need One?)

An altimeter does one simple thing: it estimates your altitude. It is just one more tool to combine with solid map-reading skills for accurate orientation and navigation. If you will be traveling in terrain that is more or less flat (less than 500 feet of total elevation change in a travel day), you may not need an altimeter at all.

When you are navigating in mountainous terrain, knowing your elevation and tracking your elevation changes can be both fun and enlightening, whether you are on foot, on skis, on a bike, or in a kayak. Keeping track of your elevation and location on the map with an altimeter is one way to become familiar with the amount of time and energy it takes to climb or descend in steeper terrain. By estimating in advance how long it will take you to reach a certain elevation, then checking your actual elevation with an altimeter, you can begin to understand your group's limits and abilities. Over time, your estimations will become more and more accurate, and you will become a better navigator.

There are essentially two types of altimeters routinely used for land navigation today—barometric or true altimeters and newer GPS-based altimeters. Barometric altimeters tend to be slightly more expensive, but also more reliable. GPS-based altimeters have become a standard feature in many smart-phones, but can be inaccurate and require a cellular signal.

Barometric Altimeters

Barometers are instruments that measure the weight of air. They give an air pressure reading in measurements like millibars or inches of mercury. Altimeters are barometers that are calibrated to give the same air pressure measurement in terms of feet or meters above sea level. This works because as altitude increases, air pressure decreases in a constant manner. That means that on the summit of Mount Everest, the air pressure will always be much lower than anywhere at sea level. In fact, low air pressure is precisely why many high-altitude mountaineers use oxygen tanks and why there are emergency oxygen masks above your seat on commercial planes. Near sea level an inch of mercury is roughly equivalent to 1,000 feet of elevation.

Typical digital altimeter

Barometric altimeters are either digital or analog. Over the last decade, digital barometric altimeters have made their way into handheld GPS units and many watches designed for outdoor use. They are surprisingly accurate when used properly, and because they are part of your watch or GPS, they are harder to lose than the standalone versions. Most altimeter watches will also display the temperature and your rate of ascent or descent. Some feature alarms that can be set to go off at a certain elevation and log books that will automatically record your altitude changes for review later.

There are two distinct disadvantages to using digital altimeters: they are more affected by extreme temperatures, and there is always the risk of the battery dying when you need it most. Most models are inoperable below -5°F. (-20°C) or above 120°F. (50°C). This temperature limitation will probably not affect an altimeter watch as long as it stays on your wrist. (If the temperature on your wrist is below -5°F or above 120°F, you have more important problems than figuring out your elevation.) If you need to take the watch off in extreme temperatures, keep it in an inside pocket. Most models will retain altitude information even if the LCD screen goes blank in cold temperatures. On longer expeditions, make sure you change your altimeter's battery before you go, or take a spare and know how to change it. Be wary of models that will ask you not to change the battery yourself.

Typical analog altimeter

If you are wondering what digital altimeter brands to buy, Suunto, Silva, Casio, Garmin, and Timex all produce several models that are quite accurate when reset regularly. Before you rush out to buy one, consider what other features you may want (heart rate monitor, GPS, compass, and so on) and how easily it will sync with your computer's operating system.

Analog altimeters have faded from use for land navigation by all but a handful of high-altitude mountaineers, scientists, and polar explorers. They still work well at subfreezing temperatures and have fewer parts to break or malfunction. They are also very easy to use. They resemble and are carried like a pocket watch. If you're looking to stay below 16,000 feet, there are several analog models under $100. Otherwise, digital may be the way to go. To read an analog altimeter, give it a couple of light taps to loosen the needle, then look straight down on it rather than at an angle.

CONSIDERATIONS FOR USING BAROMETRIC ALTIMETERS

As the weather changes, the air pressure changes, which can throw off your altimeter. For example, you may be in camp all day while a low-pressure system moves into your area, causing your altimeter to read several hundred feet higher by the end of the day. One way to overcome this problem is by resetting your reference altitude. When you are at a known elevation like a trail intersection, summit, or lake, double-check your altimeter's reading and adjust it to match the altitude you have for your location on the map. In periods of stable weather, you may not need to reset for several days. Of course, getting a good reading will be most important in bad weather, when visibility is low. Take the time to check the accuracy of your altitude and reset each night in camp when elevation details are critical.

The designers of digital altimeters have tried several ways to lessen the effects of changing weather readings. Some allow you to turn off the altimeter while you are in camp so that the watch registers the air pressure changes on the barometer, but not on the altimeter. This works well as long as you remember to turn it off each night and back on again before you leave camp. Some altimeters with integrated GPS units can distinguish between changes in elevation (location) and changes in weather, limiting the need to reset. If your altimeter doesn't talk directly to a GPS, expect to either turn off the altimeter or reset it at least once daily in the mountains.

The temperature may also have an adverse effect on your altimeter reading. As the temperature rises and falls, the altimeter's sensor expands and contracts, leading to inaccuracies.

The good news is that most altimeters made within the last decade have a temperature compensation feature that works well when you are not changing elevation. When you are changing elevation and the temperature swings rapidly, there can still be minor problems with even temperature-compensated models. As mentioned above, keeping the altimeter on your wrist or inside your layers while you are moving helps it to stay at a fairly even temperature. Body heat is enough to counter the effects of temperature change in all but very extreme situations.

BASIC WEATHER FORECASTING
WITH BAROMETRIC ALTIMETERS

If you intend to be an expert wilderness navigator, you need to have a basic understanding of meteorology. In particular, you should be able to recognize the difference between local daily weather patterns and potentially dangerous frontal systems. If you have a good grasp on the basics, your altimeter can help you predict weather changes.

Spending a day or two at base camp watching the weather and keeping an eye on your altimeter when visiting a new area can be enlightening. As air pressure drops, the altimeter reading goes up and the barometer reading goes down. If your elevation is not changing, but the altitude goes up on your altimeter, there is probably a low-pressure system moving into your area. Meteorology is a complex science, but in general, lower pressure means more unstable weather. Conversely, if the altimeter is reading a lower elevation, the air pressure is increasing—usually a sign of stabilizing weather.

Bad weather with minimal change in pressure usually means that it's part of the regular local weather patterns, whereas bad weather with a change in pressure probably signals a front moving in. In order to really develop an eye for weather patterns in a given area, you will have to spend some time in the field and monitor your altimeter and barometer readings as the weather changes. Most areas of the tropics, for example, experience alternating rainy seasons (when it is mostly hot and sunny, with brief rains almost every day for several months) and dry seasons (when it is overcast and cooler but doesn't rain at all).

Being able to determine the difference between daily weather patterns and frontal systems can help you guess how long a period of bad weather may last or how severe it may be. Wherever you go, plan your route with the local weather in mind, or suffer the consequences.

GPS-Based Altimeters

For a full discussion of handheld GPS units and how the Global Positioning System works, see chapter 6.

The number of smartphone applications that provide elevation information based on your GPS location data is stunning. There are also barometer apps; however, these are not to be confused with actual barometric altimeters. The current generation of smartphones does not have barometric instrumentation. Instead, these apps work by using your GPS location and displaying air pressure data pulled from the Internet. Without the Internet connection (Wifi, 3G, 4G LTE, or EDGE), these apps cannot display your elevation accurately. So today in 2013, no cellular service means no working altimeter on your smartphone. Nonetheless, for those whose dayhikes or even camping trips will involve visiting one of the increasing number of wilderness areas where reliable cell service is available, there is no need to purchase another gadget. Additionally, industry analysts are saying that some next-generation smartphones will have real barometric altimeters.

Orienting Yourself with an Altimeter

Knowing your elevation can play a big part in determining your location. If you are on a line feature, such as a ridge, trail, or drainage, you may be able to locate yourself on the map by simply finding where the contour line at your elevation intersects the line feature you are following. In areas with few land features or low visibility (such as a dense forest), this may be the only way to locate yourself accurately. The more mountainous the terrain, the more certain you can be of your location. In rolling hills or flat terrain where the elevation is more consistent, an altimeter will be of less use.

You can also determine your location in low-visibility conditions in the mountains by simply knowing the bearing of the

In the mountains, you can use an altimeter to find your location on a trail by finding where your contour intersects the trail.

slope you are on and your elevation. Use your compass to determine in which direction the slope you are on rises and descends. Even in low visibility, you should be able to determine which slope you are on by finding the one with the same bearing on your map. Then get an accurate altimeter reading for your elevation. You are located where your elevation contour crosses the slope you have identified.

Exercise 1: Tracking Elevation Changes

While in the backcountry, check your altitude at campsites, lakes, trail intersections, and other known elevations for several days in a row. How often do you need to reset your reference altitude? How accurate is it? Record any differences in your altimeter reading and known elevation several times each day. Can you determine a typical margin of error for your altimeter? Are the weather changes you see consistent with changes in the barometer?

Exercise 2: Watching the Weather

For the next few weeks, keep a weather journal for the area that you're in. Take a few minutes each day to write down the following weather observations:

- What cloud types do you see? How are they changing? Are the changes consistent with the usual daily patterns?
- What are the wind speed and wind direction on the ground? Are they changing? Do the clouds seem to be moving with the same speed and in the same direction?
- What is the current temperature? Is it trending above or below the normal daily fluctuations?

- What is the air pressure? Is it typical for the elevation in your location? Is it changing?

Weather observations are most significant in the context of patterns over time, which often don't emerge without at least a few days of weather watching. How do the data entries you've recorded compare? How is it different in various locations? At different times of the day? Different times of the year? What relationships do you find between changes in air pressure and weather patterns?

CHAPTER 5 | COORDINATE SYSTEMS

Imagine that you are an emergency dispatcher for a search-and-rescue team with a rescue helicopter in the northwestern United States. A call comes in about a serious accident on a wilderness trip. The caller is using a satellite phone without GPS or other locator technology. Someone has fallen and needs immediate medical attention. Your job is to determine the exact location of the injured person so that you can dispatch a rescue helicopter to that location. Time is critical.

Them: We've had an accident about five miles north of Badger Lake. My friend hurt his leg and is bleeding all over the place! We need a helicopter!

You: Are you calling from Oregon or Washington?

Them: Oregon . . . Near Mount Hood.

You: Do you know your numerical coordinates?

Them: Well, no. But I know where we are on the map.

You: Can you tell me what map are you using?

Them: Uh . . . It's the "Green Trails" map of Mount Hood, Oregon, #462.

You: Are you within a mile of any distinct land feature that is named on the map?

Them: Well, we're about two miles from Trail 650, but it turns into trail 480 farther down.

You: Which direction is Trail 650 from where you are?

Them: Kind of southwest, but really more west than south, I guess.

You: What is the distance and direction of Mount Hood from your current location?

Them: Well, actually, it's on the other map. I'll have to grab it out of the tent. Hold on a minute . . . [several minutes pass] . . . OK . . . Uh . . . it's about eight miles west of here.

You: So, you are eight miles east of Mount Hood, five miles north of Badger Lake, and two miles east-northeast of Trail 650. Is that right?

Them: That sounds right, but . . . Gosh, I'm sorry—I meant to say south of Badger Lake. Can you guys hurry up? My buddy has lost a lot of blood and really needs help fast!

Coordinates take the guesswork out of describing locations. Rather than using land features and triangulation to describe an area, coordinates pinpoint a precise location. By carefully locating a point within a grid on a map, navigators can reference a precise location on land or sea without relying on landmarks at all. If you ever plan to use GPS, or if there is a chance you may need to give someone your location in an emergency, you need to learn how to read and plot coordinates. This chapter will provide a basic understanding of latitude/longitude and UTM coordinate systems, teach you to determine coordinates for a known point on a map, and show you how to plot a point on the map from given coordinates.

Coordinate Systems

A coordinate system is simply a numbered grid or series of grids laid over a map. By using measurable values on the grid, you can find an exact location on the map. Most coordinate systems are based on an X axis (horizontal value) and a Y axis (vertical value). Road maps and atlases often use letters for one axis and

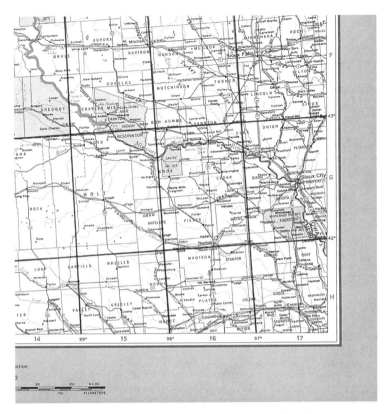

Coordinate systems are an essential part of most maps. The letter/number system shown here in this map of Nebraska and South Dakota is a common method.

numbers for another. With a checkerboard-style grid drawn over the map, coordinates such as "7C" give you a more specific area in which to search for the town or intersection you are trying to locate.

While there are a number of coordinate systems in the world, the most commonly used for land navigation are the latitude/longitude system and the Universal Transverse Mercator (UTM) system. Most topo maps are printed with coordinates from at least one system in the margin. All USGS quads feature both types of coordinates; older USGS quads will also have red township and range grids printed on them.

Plotting coordinates on a paper map is much easier with transparent map rulers that have minutes and seconds marked on them. Make sure the rulers you're using match your map scale. Some compasses have a map ruler built into the base plate. The rulers you will need for latitude/longitude measurements differ from the UTM grid readers. Some map tools feature both.

You can also find a variety of free map tools to download at www.maptools.com. Transparent plastic copies can be purchased at www.nols.edu.

UTM Coordinates

The Mercator projection, named after a sixteenth-century Flemish inventor, was created for sailors to use to determine courses. Because the UTM system is based on uniform grids of 1,000 square meters, it is considerably easier to use than latitude and longitude, which require you to use two different rulers or turn your ruler diagonally. UTM is to coordinate systems what the metric system is to measurements of distance—in fact, all measurements are in units of 10.

The UTM grid system divides the earth into zones. There are sixty primary zones that run north to south and twenty optional zones that run east to west. The primary zones are represented by numbers, while the optional zones are represented by letters. Austin, Texas, for example, is in zone 14R. The letter "R" indicates that the UTM coordinate given is located in the northern hemisphere. (Often, the letter is left off the zone description because it is not necessary.) Take a look at your map. USGS maps will list the zone

Map ruler (not to scale)

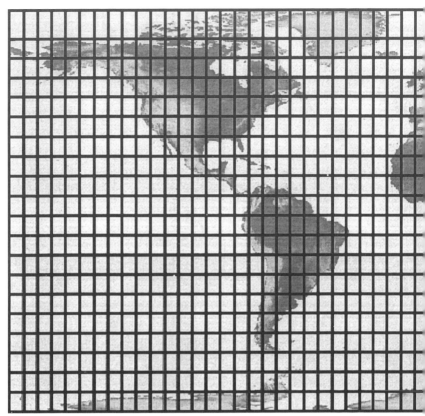

1 2 3 4 5 6 7 8 9 10 11 12 13 14 15 16 17 18 19 20 21 22 23 24 25 26 27 28 29 30

The Universal Transverse Mercator system is a coordinate system that divides the surface of the earth into a series of smaller regions.

in the text in the bottom left corner of the margin. To be perfectly clear, you should always include the zone with the UTM coordinates when you're giving your location. Which zone are you in right now?

Each zone is further divided into numbered grids, each one representing a square kilometer. Each of these UTM grids is expressed in units of meters, with a particular point on the grid specified as the number of meters east and north in that zone—

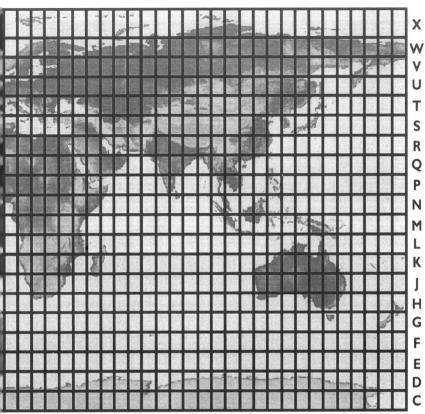

32 33 34 35 36 37 38 39 40 41 42 43 44 45 46 47 48 49 50 51 52 53 54 55 56 57 58 59 60

these are called the "easting" and "northing" values. The full-length version of these values is located on the top left and bottom right borders of each USGS quad. Take a moment now to locate them on your map. They follow this format: 442000mE, 3665000mN. The digits that represent thousands of meters and tens of thousands of meters are enlarged to help you quickly locate which kilometer reference lines to use.

Although some newer USGS quads come with printed UTM grid lines, most do not. In order to more accurately plot coordinates, you can draw these lines on your map. UTM tick marks

are printed in blue along the border and usually have a corresponding number in black next to each tick. A 24-inch ruler can
be used to draw grid lines connecting these ticks. To draw lines
in the field, you can also
fold the edge of the map
over to use as an impromptu
straightedge.

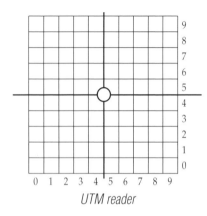

UTM reader

In order to read and plot
UTM coordinates, you must
have a UTM grid reader that
matches the scale of the map
(1:24,000 for USGS quads). In
a pinch, grid readers can be
made in the field by transferring the 100-meter marks from
the map's metric distance scale to the upper right corner of a
straight-edged piece of paper.

DETERMINING UTM COORDINATES
FROM A POINT ON THE MAP

To read the UTM coordinates for a known point "X" on the map,
place the grid reader directly over the grid where X is located.
Read the easting value first. Start from the closest vertical gridline to the left (west) of the X; in the diagram to the right, this is
581000mE. To get the easting coordinate for the X, simply add
the number of 100-meter squares you count to X from the vertical gridline. In this case, the number of squares is two, so the
easting value is 581200m.E. You read the northing value by
counting up from the lower (southern) horizontal gridline. Here,
the northing value for X is 5390800mN. The easting and northing values give you your location to the nearest 100 meters,
plus or minus 50 meters (half a soccer field).

To be more precise, you can read to 10-meter increments.
Imagine ten tick marks along the bottom of the 100-meter

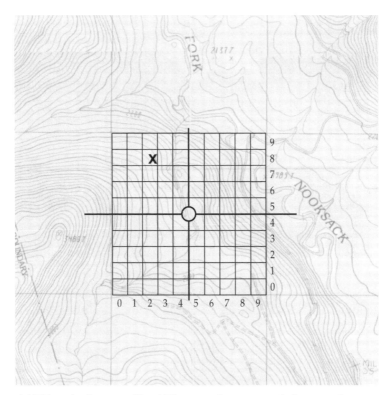

*A UTM reader lines up with grid lines on a topo map and allows you to reference an exact location in the UTM system. In this example from the USGS quad for Twin Sisters Mountain in Washington State, the coordinates of the X within this UTM grid are approximately 200mE, 800mN. (The full coordinates are **581**200mE, 53**90**800mN.)*

square surrounding X. The center of X is about seven ticks to the right of the "2" line. The precise easting value is therefore 581270mE.

PLOTTING A POINT ON THE MAP
FROM UTM COORDINATES

To plot a point on the map from given coordinates, simply reverse the process for reading. Start by placing the grid reader on the right of the corresponding vertical gridline. Then, keeping the reader on that gridline, move it vertically up or down the map until it is on the correct horizontal gridline. Count the correct number of 100-meter squares in from both gridlines and, looking through the grid reader, visualize the point you wish to mark on the map. Then move the grid reader and mark the X. Lastly, reposition the grid reader and double-check your mark.

Latitude and Longitude

The latitude/longitude system was the first widely used coordinate system in the world. Created by the ancient scholar Ptolemy around two thousand years ago, latitude/longitude coordinates are still used by pilots, sailors, land management agencies, and many GPS users. While they are slightly more cumbersome to use than UTM coordinates, wilderness navigators in North America should understand latitude/longitude coordinates and be able to determine them in an emergency.

Like UTM, the latitude/longitude coordinate system is used to indicate an exact physical location on Earth with numbers. Latitude and longitude are measured in degrees, minutes, and seconds. These may sound like time measurements, but they're not. Cartographers (mapmakers) divide the Earth into 360 degrees. Each degree is subdivided into 60 minutes, and each minute is subdivided into 60 seconds. Rather than dividing minutes into 60 parts to get seconds, some navigators prefer to measure in tenths of minutes. Forty-two minutes, thirty seconds (42'30") equals forty-two-point-five minutes (42.5'). The 1:24,000-scale maps have a height of 7.5 minutes of latitude and a width of 7.5 minutes of longitude, and they are called 7.5-minute series maps. If you look at a 7.5-minute USGS map, you'll see measurements of latitude and longitude in the mar-

Lines of longitude (left) and latitude (right).

gins at 2.5-minute intervals. Measurements of latitude appear as black ticks in the left and right margins, and measurements of longitude appear on the top and bottom. Within the frame of the map, four small black crosses appear where the lines of latitude and longitude intersect. They look like tiny crosshairs you would see through a rifle scope. These marks make drawing in latitude and longitude lines very easy.

DETERMINING LATITUDE OF A KNOWN POINT ON THE MAP

Latitude represents a north-south position on Earth. In other words, as you go north or south, your latitude changes. Lines of latitude are parallel to one another and evenly spaced—in fact, they are also called parallels. So, a degree of latitude represents a constant distance on the ground.

To determine latitude from a known point, orient a map ruler vertically (north to south) so that it spans the lines of latitude that the point falls between. When you're in the northern hemisphere, the zero-minute end of the ruler should be on the

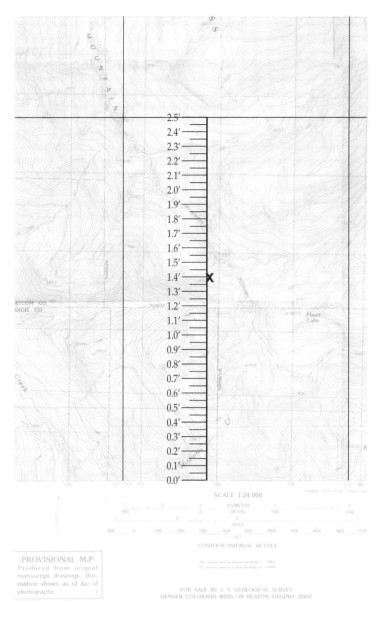

The X lies 1.4 minutes north of the 48°37'30" line on the Twin Sisters map, giving it a latitude of 48°38.9' north.

southern line of latitude. Read the value from the ruler at the given point and add it to the latitude at the zero end of the ruler. In the illustration to the left, X is at the 1.4' mark. The 0.0 mark on the ruler is at 48°37'30" or 48°37.5'. Adding 1.4' to 48°37.5' gives a resulting latitude of 48 degrees, 38.9 minutes north.

DETERMINING LONGITUDE OF A KNOWN POINT ON THE MAP

Longitude represents an east-west position on Earth. Lines of longitude are called meridians. Longitude changes as you move east or west of the Prime Meridian, which crosses Greenwich, England, and has a longitude of 0 degrees. Because the lines of longitude converge at the poles, a degree of longitude is not a constant distance on the ground—if you look at a globe with latitude and longitude marked, you'll see that longitude lines are much closer together near the poles than on the equator. This makes measuring longitude a bit trickier than measuring latitude!

You must hold the map ruler diagonally to measure longitude. Place it so that it spans the lines of longitude with the point to be measured between. The zero end of the ruler should be touching one meridian, and the 2.5' line should be touching the other one. (Remember, there are 2.5 minutes between meridians on the USGS quad.) You may need to extend the longitude lines above or below the map to properly position the ruler. Slide the ruler vertically toward the point, keeping each end on a line of longitude. Keep sliding until the edge of the ruler touches the point to be measured. If you can't get the ruler in the right position, try rotating it 90 degrees to switch the ends. In the example, X is at 1.47' on the map ruler. Adding 1.47' to 121°55' gives a resulting longitude of 121 degrees, 56.47 minutes west.

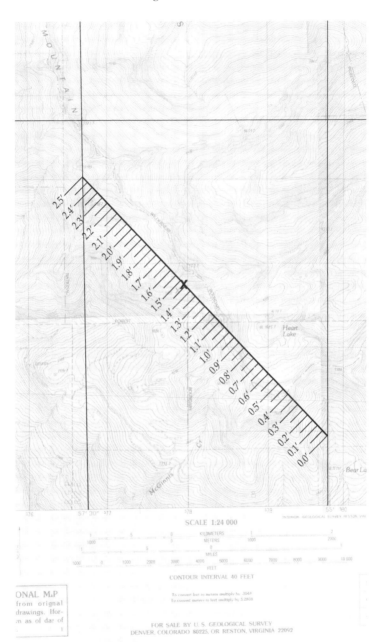

The X lies 1.47 minutes west of the 121°55' line, giving it an approximate longitude of 121°56.47' west.

PLOTTING A POINT ON THE MAP FROM LATITUDE AND LONGITUDE

To plot the location of given coordinates, first find the latitude by measuring up from the southern gridline and making a small line on the map that is parallel to the other lines of latitude. Then plot the longitude coordinate. The best way to do this is to put your map ruler between two of the map's meridians, make a small tick at the correct longitude, then move the ruler vertically and make another tick. Connecting the two ticks should give you a line that lies along the given line of longitude, at the correct angle. Double-check your marks, then extend those lines using a straight-edge and a light pencil. The point is where the plotted lines of latitude and longitude intersect.

Township and Range Lines

Many USGS maps still feature red grid lines that depict the US Public Land Survey. These lines divide land into square-mile sections but rarely run from true north to south. (Do not use them for compass work.) Thirty-six of these sections form a six-mile-square area called a township. The horizontal lines that border the township are called township lines, while the vertical lines are called range lines. If you take a look at a USGS quad, you'll notice that the sections are numbered in red in a rather odd back-and-forth pattern.

6	5	4	3	2	1
7	8	9	10	11	12
18	17	16	15	14	13
19	20	21	22	23	24
30	29	28	27	26	25
31	32	33	34	35	36

Township and range grids are rarely used for navigational purposes today. They can come in handy, however, if you don't have the time or tools to determine coordinates but need to describe an exact location. To give an example, I was recently involved in a search for a

All township grids follow this configuration.

group of five lost teenagers. As our search team was driving to the trailhead to begin searching a likely area, a search plane spotted the lost party from the air and contacted us by air-to-ground radio: "They are in Township 22 North on the high point directly between section 32 and section 33." We could immediately mark their location on our map, and we found the lost group just two hours later.

Converting Coordinates

If you find yourself needing to convert coordinates from UTM to latitude/longitude or vice versa, there are several easy solutions. The first is to use a GPS receiver—see chapter 6 for a detailed explanation. Another is to use an online conversion website. Here are a couple that convert coordinates:

http://gis.dep.wv.gov/convert/llutm_conus.php
http://www.ngs.noaa.gov/TOOLS/utm.shtml

Exercise 1: Determining Coordinates Given a Point on a Map

Mark a point in each quadrant of your map. Using a map ruler and a grid reader, determine both the latitude and longitude as well as the UTM coordinates for each point. Have another person double-check your coordinates by erasing your marks and having them plot the coordinates you give them.

Exercise 2: Determining Coordinates without Map Tools

Once you have had some practice with grid readers and map rulers, test your ability to estimate a position on the map. In *non-emergency situations* where accuracy is less critical, you may choose to "eyeball" coordinates and work without map tools. Pick a couple of spots on your map and try to determine coordinates for those locations by sight. After you have written down your eyeball estimates, double-check them using a grid reader or map ruler. How close were you?

Conclusion

If plotting coordinates seems tedious, that's because it is at first. But after a few successful attempts, it can become routine. While knowing how to manually plot coordinates is still an important skill to have, digital map software and GPS are making the process of plotting coordinates on paper maps much less common. But, watch out! Murphy's Law dictates that the one time you really need to call in your coordinates for an emergency, your GPS will have just used up your spare set of batteries.

CHAPTER 6 | GPS

If you can think of your compass as a bicycle for a moment, a handheld GPS is more like motorcycle. It can take you a long distance with less effort, but it has more parts that can break down—and it runs out of power after being used for a while. It's also quite a bit more expensive and comes with a bigger owner's manual. And just as on a motorcycle you don't get the same sort of exercise you do on a bicycle, the muscle between your ears will get less of a workout if you navigate exclusively by GPS. So here's the big question: If you were going on a long motorcycle trip and could carry your bicycle in your pocket, wouldn't you?

Today, it is still foolish to head days-deep into the backcountry without a map and compass—GPS or no GPS. Electronic things, just like motorized things, can and do break. A GPS or smartphone is not a replacement for good map skills or a shortcut to the backcountry. Learn to read a topographic map and use a compass before relying on electronics to tell you where to go. The search-and-rescue stories of GPS users who didn't have adequate navigation skills or were not even carrying a topo map when they were finally found have been adding up over the last decade. Please, please, please, don't become one of them. If you really want to become a competent land navigator, use your map and compass to navigate and only use the GPS to track, mark a waypoint, or travel in low visibility situations. Whether you have a GPS receiver or not, learn to read the terrain and *always* bring along your map and compass.

What Is GPS?

The Global Positioning System is a network of satellites orbiting the earth broadcasting radio signals. A handheld GPS receiver is a small gadget that can read the radio signals from the satellites and determine your location anywhere on earth. While the letters "G-P-S" actually refer to the whole system of satellites, radio towers, and receivers, users commonly refer to the GPS receiver they hold in their hand as a "GPS" or simply a "handheld." To further complicate usage of the term, "GPS" is becoming more commonly used to also refer to the US-launched satellite constellations as opposed to "GLONASS," the Russian-launched satellite constellation. Many newer handhelds and smartphones

GPS technology depends on a network of satellites orbiting the Earth.

A Brief History of GPS

In the early 1970s, the US Department of Defense launched the first GPS satellites. Initially, their primary use was for weapons-system targeting—more satellites in the sky meant more consistent accuracy. The US military coordinated satellite launches and eventually planned the satellite constellation known as NAVSTAR (Navigation Satellite Timing and Ranging). With each new satellite, the signals became more consistent and accurate. By 1994, a full twenty-four satellites were in place and NAVSTAR became fully operational.

Today, the NAVSTAR satellites orbit the Earth on one of six different paths. At about 12,500 miles above Earth, they move at 7,000 miles per hour, completing a full orbit each twelve hours. On a clear night, outside of population centers, they are easily visible with the naked eye. The current satellites are replaced about every ten years. They are solar-powered and consist of a computer, a radio transmitter, and an extremely accurate atomic clock. Government-monitored ground stations track them and keep them in the proper orbit.

GPS receivers need to be able to track the signal from at least four satellites at one time in order to be accurate. They determine position by measuring and comparing the time it takes radio signals to travel from each satellite down to the receiver. In GPS geek-speak, the satellites are the "space segment," the ground stations make up the "control segment," and those of us moving around on the surface make up the "user segment."

The first handheld GPS receivers were introduced in 1989. At that time, the DOD was concerned about the high level of accuracy of this new technology, which was becoming widely available. The government introduced "Selective Availability" (SA) by purposefully adding errors into NAVSTAR data to reduce accuracy of civilian GPS units to 100 meters. By 1998, handheld receivers were accurate within 100 feet 95 percent of the time if SA was turned off. As commercial uses for GPS

A Brief History of GPS *continued*

developed, pressure increased to do away with SA. On May 2, 2000, Selective Availability was turned off permanently in the United States and the accuracy of civilian GPS units went from within 300 feet to less than 50 feet. Even more accurate is the Wide Area Augmentation System (WAAS), a Federal Aviation Administration system that combines data from ground stations with satellite data to increase GPS accuracy. WAAS-activated GPS receivers are accurate to within 10 feet. (On the downside, they are more expensive and use more batteries, though some units allow the WAAS feature to be turned on and off.) These advances in accuracy coincided with a boom in GPS sales and applications.

In war zones, the DOD may still jam GPS signals to prevent enemies from using commercial receivers. In recent years, controversy has raged over the deployment of the European Union's own GPS satellite system, "Galileo." If it ever becomes operational, Galileo will have thirty satellites and allow for accuracy to within 3 feet. Obviously, the United States will be less able to selectively degrade signals from this new system.

use both the U.S. and Russian satellites, improving their speed and accuracy.

Because a GPS can keep track of time and your location, it can use that data to provide you with some important information:

- Your current location coordinates
- Your altitude (though not usually as accurate as a properly used barometric altimeter)
- Your speed—average, maximum, and current
- Your distance traveled
- Your estimated time of arrival at a known destination

- Your current heading or direction of travel (only while you are moving)
- The bearing to your destination (only while you are moving)
- The bearing to any previous destination—you should be able to retrace your steps at any time using the tracking feature.

Depending on the features of the model you have and how it may integrate with map software, there are a number of other things GPS can do for you, including giving you a real-time display of your current location right on your device.

There are a growing number of handheld and wrist-top GPS units available today. This chapter focuses on commonalities between most recreational GPS units and gives an idea of how GPS receivers work. Think of the suggestions here as a supplement to your manufacturer's user manual. Yes . . . you still have to read the manual.

Who Should Buy a GPS?

Today, asking yourself if you need a handheld GPS for backcountry travel is still a worthwhile thing to do. Prices are still high enough to warrant some consideration, and many folks venture into the wilderness precisely to get away from the digital screens that we tend to spend so much time staring at. Despite what commercials and magazine advertisements will tell you, not every backcountry traveler needs a handheld GPS! Whether you should purchase a GPS unit depends on where you will be traveling and for what purpose. It also depends on what other gadgets you have in your toolbox. That is because so many outdoor electronics today already have integrated GPS technology: smartphones, two-way radios, cameras, and even ski goggles. GPS units really come into use during navigation in featureless terrain like oceans, deserts, and polar regions. They also work wonders in low-visibility conditions like traveling at night or in nasty storms.

Here are a few questions to aid your decision: Will you be traveling for extended periods of time in areas where the terrain is difficult to see? What are the consequences of being disoriented in the areas you are planning to visit? Will you be sticking to shorter trips into the mountains or canyons? Do new toys excite you or do they seem like one more thing to lug along or lose? Will you be spending most of your time in the jungle under a dense tree canopy, or in another environment where GPS may not work very well? Is it important to know your exact speed and distance traveled? Do you already own a GPS-enabled smartphone AND have the ability to recharge in the field?

Operating a GPS

GETTING THE RIGHT SETTINGS

Before getting started, you have to make sure you, your map, and your GPS are speaking the same language. If not, you are headed for some miscommunication and probably some bad directions. Take some time to get your settings correct each time you are traveling to a new area.

The Earth is not a perfectly round sphere. It actually has an irregular ellipsoid shape, which makes creating a very accurate two-dimensional map fairly complicated. The map datum is the mathematical model that corresponds to the shape of the Earth. There are more than one hundred sets of map datum made from different mathematical measurements around the Earth, and each map series has its own datum. What all of this means for you is you must always make sure the datum setting in your

GPS matches the datum on your map. If your GPS is using the wrong datum for the map you are using, your GPS coordinates may be hundreds of meters off. On a USGS quad, the datum is in the margin at the bottom left-hand corner, near the UTM zone. Luckily, most quads use either the World Grid System of 1984 Datum (WGS 84) or the North American Datum of 1927 (NAD 27). By default, GPS receivers use the WGS 84 Datum. A common mistake is to use NAD 27 map data without setting your GPS to that datum, which can direct you up to 800 feet in the wrong direction. Many people also forget to change the datum setting when they travel internationally.

Another setting to check is your position format. Position format is the coordinate system in which you would like the GPS to display your location. You can choose UTM, several versions of latitude/longitude, or one of many other options. Unless you are traveling in one of the polar regions, UTM or latitude/longitude will suit your recreational needs. On the position format screen, there may be several options for how to view your latitude and longitude. You can choose degrees, minutes, and seconds (D,M,S); degrees and decimal minutes (D,M.M); or decimal degrees (D.DD). Which option you choose is not nearly as important as knowing how to measure it on your map. Pick the display to which your map ruler is calibrated.

Yet another setting to consider is metric/statute distances. This choice should be based simply on which system you are most comfortable with and what is on your map. Statute distances are given in miles, yards, and feet; metric distances are in kilometers and meters. Generally, it's best to have your GPS set according to whatever units are displayed on your map.

If all this seems a bit complex, relax—you won't need to change your settings every time you go out. Unless you're a jet setter, you'll probably even be using the same map datum most or all of the time.

ACQUIRING SIGNALS

When you turn your GPS on for the first time in a new area, it will take a few minutes to acquire satellite signals. Most units will acquire signals within a minute or so after being turned on, though this process can take up to five minutes if the GPS is in a completely new area or does not have a clear view of the sky. While it will work in most tree cover, it generally won't work well inside a building or under a very dense tree canopy, like that of a tropical jungle.

Your GPS will give you an estimated degree of accuracy as it acquires and loses satellite signals. With current technology and NAVSTAR satellites, recreational GPS receivers will only be accurate to within about 30 feet. Your GPS may claim to be more accurate, but don't bet your life on it. When you add in the human error factor, getting within 30 feet of your target is actually quite remarkable. And unless you are literally looking for a needle in a haystack, 30 feet should be as close as you need to get to see your objective. A tent, a pond, a trail junction, a car, a bicycle, and even a baseball are visible from 30 feet in most terrain. If you are navigating with your GPS, it is smart to start to slow down and look for your objective once the GPS says you are within 100 feet.

Once the GPS has acquired several satellite signals, it can give you your current position. This is called getting a position fix.

WAYPOINTS

A waypoint is GPS lingo for a specific location that is stored in your GPS. You can have your GPS mark a waypoint at anytime, anywhere you have a signal. You can use waypoints to mark your current location, in case you want to return later or track where you've been on a map.

There may also be times when you would like to enter the coordinates for a location you have never visited and ask the

GPS to direct you to that location. This is how the military sends precision "smart bombs" to their targets and how geocachers locate caches. (See the geocaching exercise at the end of this chapter.) You must first determine the coordinates you would like to enter, which means either plotting them on your topo map as explained in Chapter 5, or using Google Earth or offline map software with your GPS connected to your computer. If you are using UTM coordinates, be sure you've entered the correct zone.

The GPS will automatically remember the waypoint and assign it a numerical name (001, 002, etc.) unless you rename it. It is wise to give each waypoint a unique name that will not be confusing later: Car, Camp 1, Fishing Spot 4/25/2013, Waterfall, etc. The best names combine something unique about the location with the date or sequence visited.

THE GOTO FUNCTION

Once you have waypoints recorded in the GPS, you can ask it to point you directly to any waypoint at any time by using the "Goto" function. The unit will display an arrow that points directly at the waypoint and tell you your current distance from the waypoint.

Remember, however, that you may still have some route-finding to do. The GPS may be telling you that your waypoint is only two miles south of your current location, but it will not tell you that you need to cross a 3,000-foot canyon or that a bridge is out. As always, the most direct route may or may not be the best route.

The display arrow on a GPS does not work like the magnetic needle on your compass. Unless you have a unit with a built-in digital compass, the GPS cannot determine which way it is oriented when it is sitting still. *You must be moving for the arrow to be accurate.* That means that any time you are routefinding with your GPS, you must be walking and looking at the display screen at the same time. Don't trip over that rock!

The advantage of routefinding with a GPS is that it is easy to go around obstacles (like a lake or a boulder field) and get right back on your bearing. The display arrow will always adjust to your current location to point directly toward your target. Gone is the need to make 90-degree turns and count steps off your bearing.

On longer treks you can save batteries by using the GPS to get your direction, sighting a landmark with your compass, turning the GPS off, and following the bearing with your compass. Stay on the compass bearing until you have another big obstacle to go around and need to change your heading. Remember not to set a bearing with the compass right next to the GPS—the metallic parts and batteries in the GPS will throw off the compass needle! Keep the compass and GPS at least six inches apart when you are using the compass.

TRACKING

Most handheld GPS units today feature automatic tracking. This means you can set the GPS to automatically mark points at intervals according to either distance or time. All you have to do is leave the GPS on and let it mark points for you. You can then use the "pan track" feature to scroll back in time to any location you have visited. Many units also have a "track-back" feature that enables the GPS to direct you back along your tracks. This means that if you are following a difficult route in low visibility or in an emergency you can ask the GPS to guide you in retracing your steps—think of needing to return to a scarce water source in canyon country, or to base camp when a blizzard hits in the mountains. If you have a computer connection, you can even download your tracks onto a digital topographic map and see exactly where you've been.

While using the tracking feature has a number of advantages, if you pass through dense brush while your GPS is tracking, it may drop a few of the tracks due to a weak satellite signal. Tracking also requires a lot more batteries than turning the unit on occasionally to check your current location. If you use tracking, have plenty of extra batteries on hand, or the means to recharge.

Choosing the Right GPS

The market for handheld GPS units used for wilderness navigation seems to be constantly changing. Like other outdoor toys, they are getting smaller, lighter, more specialized, and thankfully easier to use. Which one you choose to buy depends largely on how you answer these questions:

What is the main activity you will be doing with GPS?
Some models offer specialized features for cycling, running, hunting, fishing, climbing, or geocaching. For athletes, special software is available for monitoring your training. As more units hit the market, consumers will need to be careful not to buy one that is so specialized that it can't meet all their needs. If you are looking for something strictly for alerting the authorities in an emergency rather than a navigation tool, you might consider a satellite messenger or personal locator beacon. See chapter 7 for a full discussion of emergency communication.

Do you own a GPS-enabled smartphone?
If you own a smartphone, you might be better off just purchasing an application that will enable you to use the phone's GPS hardware. But using the GPS will drain the phone's battery charge fast. So if you plan on using the smartphone on extended wilderness trips, you will need a system for recharging. See

Typical handheld mapping GPS unit and wristwatch GPS (not to scale)

chapter 8 for a more complete discussion of navigation apps and portable power options.

How much can you spend?

Recreational GPS units range in price from around $70 to $800, depending on features. If you need to save some coin, come up with a list of "must have" features and resist the temptation to buy more than you can afford.

Accuracy of about 50 feet is standard for today's recreational model GPS units. Newer models featuring Wide Area Augmentation System (WAAS) or Differential GPS capabilities are accurate to within just 10 feet on average. Unless you are buying a professional-grade GPS unit (for surveying or GIS integration), more money does not necessarily mean more accuracy.

Handheld or wrist-top?

For many people on the move, a wrist-top computer or smartwatch is a good tool for wilderness travel. If your watch tells you your heart rate, altitude, air temperature, speed, and location along with the time, it's clearly more than the windup watch your grandpa wore. There are several considerations in deciding whether to choose a wrist-top or handheld model. If you're planning to do any long-distance running, adventure racing, or fast-packing with your GPS, then size and weight are important, and a wrist-top may be the way to go. If you don't see yourself ever racing along, consider a handheld GPS or smartphone instead—they are generally more user-friendly, with more features and a slightly larger size that makes it easier to manually enter data. If you want to be able to see a digital map on your GPS, you will need a handheld or smartphone. Also, if you will be entering waypoints in the field, the tiny buttons on wrist-tops can be tedious, though you may still be able to enter routes and waypoints into some wrist-tops by uploading them from your computer. Overall, it's important to balance ease of use with the need to save weight.

Do you need computer compatibility?
If you're not a computer person, you might save a few bucks by buying an older GPS that isn't computer-friendly. If you are, you want to make sure the software and GPS you buy will work with your computer and operating system. Most of the receivers being sold today are designed to interface with a Mac, PC, or both. See chapter 8 for more on map software.

Do you need a map display?
While all GPS receivers have some sort of display screen, not all of them can display maps. The wrist-tops and cheaper handhelds with smaller screens will not display maps. As far as digital map displays go, there are essentially three kinds of GPS units suitable for land navigation:
  • Those that display digital maps right on the unit
  • Those that don't display digital maps on the unit, but may still link up to your computer

- GPS-enabled smartphones or tablets (which typically do feature a map display)

A map display on your GPS may not be worth the extra cost and shorter battery life. Being able to see maps on your GPS screen is pretty cool, but whether you really *need* it depends in part on what kind of traveling you will be doing. Do you need to go fast and light, or are you setting up a three-week base camp somewhere?

Batteries

Whatever else you do, make sure you have enough battery power for your entire trip if you are depending on electronics for help with navigation. For most situations, that means always carrying at least one spare set. Make sure you know exactly how long a set of batteries will last in your GPS before heading into the backcountry.

When your GPS is on and operating normally, it is processing satellite signals about every second. Some handheld models will burn through a set of batteries in just three to six hours if the unit is continuously on. So keep it in battery saver mode or turned off until you really need it. Make sure, however, that you practice with it and will know how to navigate with it when the time comes. See chapter 8 for a complete discussion of GPS-enabled smartphones, battery options, and portable rechargers.

Exercise 1: Plotting Coordinates and Navigating with GPS

Find a topographic map of the area where you live or another area you know very well and plot the coordinates for a known destination within walking distance. Measure the distance on your map between you and your destination using a string and the map scale. Then enter the coordinates into your GPS and mark the destination as a waypoint.

Use the GPS to direct you toward your destination using the Goto function. What does the GPS give as the total distance? Keep an eye on the direction arrow and estimated distance as you approach your waypoint. On some GPS units, the distance will change from miles to feet (or kilometers to meters) as you get closer to your destination.

If you turn out to be off by more than 100 feet, double-check to see that you plotted the point correctly, entered it correctly, and have all of your settings correct in the GPS.

Once you've had a chance to practice using your GPS around town several times, begin plotting coordinates and using the GPS to assist in navigating off-trail to more remote locations with less visible land features. Try getting a bearing with the GPS and then following the bearing using your map and compass.

For a real challenge, try traveling at night, off-trail, with the GPS. Don't forget a partner(s) and some emergency bivouac gear.

Exercise 2: Determining Average Speed

Use your GPS to determine your average speed walking, running, or cycling. How do those averages change over different kinds of terrain (on-/off-road, on-/off-trail, up-/downhill)?

Exercise 3: Finding a Geocache

Geocaching.com describes geocaching as "a real-world outdoor treasure hunting game. Players try to locate hidden containers, called geocaches, using GPS-enabled devices and then share their experiences online." Participating in a cache hunt is a good way to take advantage of the wonderful features and capability of a GPS unit. The basic idea is to have individuals and organizations set up caches all over the world and share the locations of these caches on the Internet. GPS users can then use the location coordinates to find the caches. Once found, a cache may provide the visitor with a wide variety of rewards. All the visitor is asked to do is leave something in the cache if they take something from the cache.

A cache is a hidden container, like an army surplus ammo box, with a variety of inexpensive trinkets and a registry inside to make note of who has found it. Many geocachers document their finds on the Internet. While some caches are designed to be found by off-road vehicle users, others are hidden specifically for those on foot. Some caches are obvious once you find them, but others are cleverly disguised to look like a normal part of their environment (like a hollow rock).

To give geocaching a try, go to www.geocaching.com and enter your zip code or town name to find coordinates for a geocache near you. When you select a cache, the coordinates will appear in both UTM and latitude/longitude. Make sure you have the right map and that if you're using UTM, the datum given with the coordinates matches the datum on your map.

If you own a newer model smartphone with its own GPS hardware, consider downloading Garmin's free geocaching app, OpenCaching, for iPhone or Android. You can also purchase a variety of geocaching apps at geocaching.com.

For a more serious challenge to both your plotting and general navigation skills (as well as your patience), try to locate a geocache near you without using a GPS. By plotting coordinates manually and using your map-reading skills, you can successfully locate a geocache without GPS. However, be prepared to spend some time wandering around. If you have a GPS, take it along as a backup in case you aren't having any luck—caches are often cleverly hidden.

A few reminders about geocaching:

- Never search for or place caches in designated wilderness areas.
- Make sure you are complying with local and federal laws and not trespassing on private property.
- Don't forget to bring something to leave in the cache.

Good Luck!

LOST IN THE WILDERNESS

If you are traveling off-trail through wild areas regularly, sooner or later you will get lost. In rolling terrain, thick forest, or weather that limits visibility, even the best navigators can become disoriented. This temporary sort of confusion is normal and happens all the time. Usually, getting to a place with a better view or orienting the map with a compass is all that you need to do to relocate yourself and get back on track.

What separates the best navigators from the rest is the ability to recognize when they are starting to veer off route and to know when to simply stop and return to a known location. Making mistakes is part of navigation; refusing to admit them until it's too late, forcing your group to spend an unplanned night in the wilderness, is not. There's no shame in asking others in your group for help, but there is in silently dragging everyone fifteen miles out of their way.

Nonetheless, at some point you may become truly lost. The difference between being temporarily disoriented and being truly lost is that you aren't truly lost until you've really put some effort into locating yourself and failed. (If you're not sure where you are, but you haven't taken the time to stop and look at the map, you're not lost, just lazy.) In addition to providing tips to avoid getting truly lost, this chapter will show you how to find yourself if it happens, and how to locate others in your group if you become separated.

Prevention

People generally get truly lost in the wild because they become separated from their party, have inadequate navigation skills, or leave the map and compass behind. People who get into real trouble are those who get truly lost and don't have the right skills, food, or gear to stay alive until they are found.

BEFORE THE TRIP
A few simple trip-planning steps will make a world of difference. If you've taken the following precautions before leaving, you will be less likely to get lost—and much more at ease if you do get lost.

- Know your navigation techniques. Don't wait until you are five miles into the backcountry before learning to read a map and compass. Make sure your navigation skills are always a few notches above where they need to be for the terrain you are in. Practice in city parks or near trailheads before setting out on a multiday trip.
- Carry essential gear and extra food so that you can spend an unplanned night or two out if an emergency arises.
- For overnight trips, write a travel plan and leave it with a responsible adult. Be sure to include a detailed description of your route and return time.
- Take some time to study your route before the trip. Brief your entire group so that everyone knows what to expect.
- Have more than one navigator in your group. (What happens if the only person who knows how to read a map gets sick or injured?)

STAYING FOUND
Most people who have been lost in the wild will say they "had a feeling" they were not heading in the right direction. Why did they continue? Their answers range from "I just wasn't sure, so I

kept going" to "I didn't want to have to hike all the way back up that hill." Don't play mind games with yourself by trying to make the terrain fit the map. If you're really not sure, it's probably time to stop, tell others in your group, and get some other opinions.

There is a difference between being temporarily uncertain of your location in an area with limited visibility and being disoriented even when you can clearly see distant land features. Your job as a navigator is to make sure you don't let the first situation become the second one by panicking and plowing off course at high speed. The first thing you must do is stop and consider your options.

Imagine a continuum of certainty about your location and the direction in which you are heading. On one end of the continuum you are absolutely sure where you are and what way you're facing, like when you are standing in front of your house. On the other end, you can't recognize a single land feature and you doubt you're even on the map. As you start to slip down the continuum, you should be pulling out your compass more frequently to keep track of your direction. If you're somewhere near the middle of the continuum, it is time to turn around and

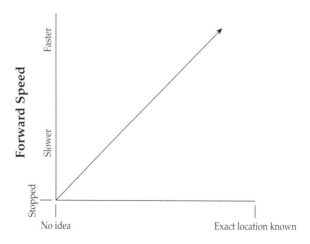

Certainty of Location

retrace your steps. By the time you've reached the truly lost end, you've likely wandered so far from your route that you might not be able to find it again.

Here are some additional tips for staying found:

- Keep everyone in your group involved in the navigation, even if they are not experts. Relying on a single person to do all the navigating for a group is usually a mistake.
- Stop and do map checks when visibility is good. Try to take breaks in areas where you have a good view so you can confirm your location.
- Look for handrails and backstops to help keep you on route.
- Keep the group together. If you have to split up, do it according to a plan, and have a contingency plan if one party doesn't make it back by a set time.
- Don't commit to a route unless you know you will be able to either retrace your footsteps or complete the route. Keep asking yourself if you truly could retrace your steps if you needed to. Never descend when you can't climb back up or climb when you can't descend unless you are absolutely sure you want to commit.
- If you'll be following the same path on the return trip, look over your shoulder on the way out to see what it will look like on the way back.
- Have a designated "sweep" person whose job it is to follow along and make sure there are no stragglers drifting too far behind the rest of the hiking group.

But What If I Really Do Get Lost?

Stop! Do not continue! Every step in the wrong direction is a step in the wrong direction. Stand still, pull out your maps, take off your pack, sit, and think. The worst thing you can possibly do is speed ahead.

Most people who are lost have a mental map of where they think they are. But that map is, of course, wrong. This is why lost people who keep moving tend to move quite far in the wrong direction. Your initial efforts toward getting found need to be about finding landmarks to get back onto the actual map, not moving quickly using your incorrect mental map.

Try not to panic, or you will waste valuable energy that could be used to determine your location. Relax—merely being lost is not an emergency. Even if you are injured, out of food, and alone in a blinding snowstorm, giving up or losing your cool will not do you or anyone else any good. What you do when you realize you are lost is what is critical to whether the situation goes from a valuable learning experience to a crisis.

Once you have calmed down, consider retracing your steps. What is the last point at which you knew exactly where you were? How long has it been since you were there? What direction have you been traveling to get to where you are? Can you reverse your course given the daylight you have left?

If there is a clearing or high point nearby where you can get your bearings, consider going there to check the maps. If you have just recently become separated from your group, don't be ashamed to yell. Smart people carry whistles for just such an occasion.

If you can retrace your steps *with certainty* to the last place where you knew your location (or, if you have become separated, the last place you saw the group), then do so. Use sticks or rocks to make arrows on the trail showing the direction you are traveling. Otherwise, sit tight until you have a plan or until a third party is able to locate you.

If your entire party gets lost near dark, stop, set camp, and get some rest. In most cases, the morning sun will go a long way toward helping you get reoriented. In hot climates, travel only during the early morning or late afternoon. In cold climates, if you are without camping gear, you may have to sleep during the day if it is too cold at night. Stay hydrated. Although it may be unpleasant, most healthy people can go at least a week without food, so make water your first priority.

In a situation where your party is lost for an extended period of time, you may need to search away from your camp for short distances to see if you can get your bearings. Send parties of two or more people if possible. Be sure to mark trees, use flagging tape, or build rock cairns as you go so that you can easily retrace your steps back to your camp. Prioritize safety above Leave No Trace concerns.

Call out for search and rescue only as a last resort. If you have a satellite phone, cell phone, or an emergency beacon, you have a responsibility to use it wisely. Unless someone in your party is truly in danger of permanent disability or death, try to get yourselves to safety without involving others. Calling in a search team is not only expensive and inconvenient for others, but potentially puts other lives at risk. Accidents, such as rescue helicopter crashes, happen. If you are in a situation that warrants calling for outside help, be aware that it can take twenty-four hours or longer to mobilize a significant search team. If you have a true crisis, call immediately.

Emergency Beacons

Today, there are two types of satellite-linked gadgets designed specifically to alert authorities to your location if you become seriously lost or injured while traveling in wilderness: satellite communicators and personal locator beacons (PLBs). Both types are increasingly popular, affordable, and easy to carry, but they are also a bit controversial. At the press of a button, handheld emergency beacons send out a distress signal from virtually anywhere on the planet. While both types have assisted in saving hundreds of lives in just the last five years, they have also led to a tremendous increase in false alarms. Emergency beacons should never be used in a location where normal EMS services can be summoned by phone.

Satellite communicators and PLBs differ in several key ways. PLBs are essentially miniature versions of the same sort of homing beacons found in aircraft (Emergency Locator Transmitters or ELTs) and in boats and ships (Emergency Position Indicating Radio Beacons or EPIRBs). PLBs operate as part of an international network of satellites, ground stations, and mission control centers developed in the early '80s with the unfortunate double acronym, COSPAS-SARSAT. COSPAS is a Russian acronym that translates to "space system for the search of vessels in distress," while SARSAT stands for Search and Rescue Satellite Aided Tracking. The American contribution to SARSAT was developed by NASA and is managed by the National Oceanic and Atmospheric Association (NOAA).

When someone activates a PLB, it sends out two separate radio signals continuously every few minutes. The first signal, on 406 MHZ, is a high-powered alert that reaches COSPAS-SARSAT satellites with encoded GPS coordinates. The alert message is relayed through ground stations until it reaches the dispatcher for the nearest search-and-rescue ground team. Once the rescuers are within a couple of miles of the PLB, they can also use a homing device to receive the second (lower-powered) radio signal on the 121.5 MHZ frequency. The encoded GPS coordinates in the first signal combined with the second homing signal add a very high level of location-specific redundancy to the PLBs effectiveness.

Satellite communicators have been in commercial use since SPOT first introduced them in 2007. Satellite communicators do not use the COSPAS-SARSAT satellite constellation, but operate through the same commercial-based Low Earth Orbit (LEO) satellite constellations used by satellite phone service providers like Globalstar and Iridium.

Satellite communicators are essentially special-function GPS receivers paired with a text-only sat phone. They calculate their position using GPS satellite signals and then send coordinates and a short data message through the sat phone network. The alert message goes to a private emergency-response center managed by the provider and is then relayed to a local SAR team dispatcher.

PLB vs. SATELLITE COMMUNICATOR

If you have decided to purchase an emergency beacon of some sort, the next question to ask yourself is whether to buy a PLB or a satellite communicator. Most PLBs serve a critical but mostly singular purpose: they tell search and rescue that you need assistance at your location. Sat communicators do that too, but they can also perform a variety of other communication functions like sending short e-mails or texts and sending friends or family your coordinates so that they can track your progress or come to your assistance without involving SAR.

Why would anyone pick a PLB and give up those extra features of a sat communicator? The three main reasons are long-term cost, reliability, and simplicity of use. Sat communicators require a service plan with a monthly or annual fee similar to cell or satellite phone service. If you plan to use the service for more than a couple of years, you would save money in the long run by carrying a PLB instead. And you have to keep up on the fees or you won't be rescued, so if you do buy a sat communicator, consider having the fee automatically deducted annually from your bank account.

PLBs have several advantages over sat communicators. The strength of the 406 MHZ PLB signal (4 to 5 watts) is at least ten times more powerful than sat communicator signals, making PLBs slightly more effective, particularly in dense tree cover and bad weather.

Although PLBs were not approved for use across the United States until 2003, the dedicated COSPAS-SARSAT system has been in use for marine and aviation emergencies since 1984. Since that system is managed and used by government agencies from many nations, it is likely to be well maintained and reliable for many decades to come. As you'll see, some sat communicators can pair with smartphones, but the pairing process and need to decode blinking lights on the devices leaves room for operator error—not ideal in a time of crisis.

If what you are really after is a pure panic button for a serious emergency, a 406MHZ PLB with GPS is hard to beat. In fact, if I was pinned under a fallen tree in the jungles of Madagascar tomorrow and I could choose which kind of emergency beacon to use, I would choose a new PLB over a new sat communicator.

CHOOSING THE RIGHT PLB

In 2009, the COSPAS-SARSAT system stopped processing distress signals from the older 121.5 and 243 MHZ frequency PLBs. Older models that use these frequencies should be retired. There are also older models available that operate on 406 MHZ but do not have GPS capability. While the non-GPS models have worked effectively for quite some time, they are not much cheaper and the extra security that GPS provides could matter. The two primary manufacturers of backpacking-sized PLBs today are McMurdo in Great Britain and ACR in the United States.

McMurdo has been manufacturing PLBs since 2000. In 2009, the small and lightweight Fast Find 200 series launched. The current backpacking beacon of choice from McMurdo is the Fast Find 210 model, which is about the size of a cell phone and sells for around $250.

ACR Cobham in Florida also manufactures a variety of PLBs for land and sea. ACR's new ResQLink technically qualifies as

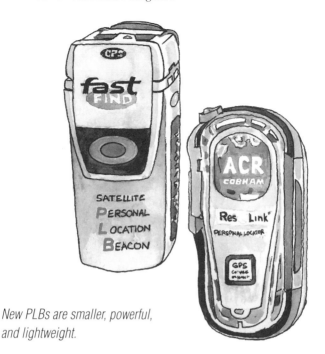

New PLBs are smaller, powerful, and lightweight.

the smallest and lightest PLB in the world at 4.6 ounces. The size and weight difference between the ResQLink and Fast Find, however, is virtually negligible. The ResQLink is slightly more powerful (+.7 watts) and slightly more waterproof (+5 minutes at 33 feet). It is also slightly more expensive (+$30). ACR offers a subscription option through 406link.com ($40 per year), which allows you to test the beacon up to twelve times using the COSPAS-SARSAT system. In an effort to compete with SPOT, a 406link Plus subscription ($60 per year) allows you to send the test message and your GPS location to five e-mail or SMS contacts.

Both McMurdo and ACR offer larger, heavier, and more expensive models that have improved power, longer battery life, and greater temperature range.

If you are considering a PLB, a few commonsense precautions will be helpful: PLBs often have a test function that allows you to check the functionality of the battery, circuitry, and antenna without sending a false alert. Batteries for PLBs last around five years if you don't use them, or 30 hours once you activate them. Use the test function and replace your batteries as needed.

By federal regulation, all PLB users in the United States must register their PLBs with NOAA at www.beaconregistration.noaa .gov. Registering the device also allows NOAA and SAR to respond to you faster in an emergency and manage false alerts more effectively. If PLBs change hands, they must be re-registered with NOAA.

CHOOSING THE RIGHT SATELLITE COMMUNICATOR

For many parts of the world, a satellite communicator will meet emergency needs and also provide some added communication features. Sat communicators offer their users the ability to send out text and e-mail messages without a cell phone signal and without a satellite phone. As with PLBs, two major manufacturers vie for top position in this new market—SPOT and Delorme. Their products have some things in common, but each also offers some unique features. Both offer standalone devices as well as devices that can pair with some smartphones. Both operate on lithium batteries that are easy to replace.

SPOT was the first to bring this technology to the masses with its first generation satellite GPS messenger in 2007. Louisiana-based SPOT is a subsidiary of Globalstar, which owns the Globalstar satellite constellation and offers a variety of satellite phone services. SPOT now offers two devices for land-based wilderness travelers: the SPOT Connect ($150) and the SPOT Satellite GPS messenger ($100). Both SPOT gadgets perform three main functions: they send an emergency SOS alert for critical incidents, they allow you to request help from friends or family for noncritical incidents, and they allow for check-in, sending e-mail or SMS messages and GPS coordinates along

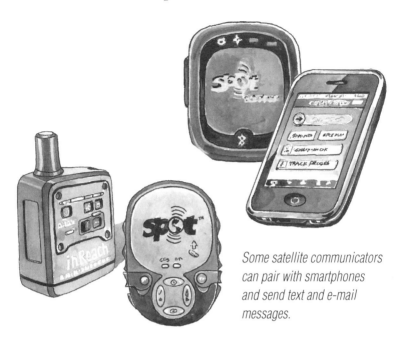

Some satellite communicators can pair with smartphones and send text and e-mail messages.

with a predetermined message and a link to Google maps showing your location. Both gadgets also require a $100 annual fee to activate. On top of the annual fee, users have the option to purchase additional services like web-based GPS tracking, type and send messaging, roadside assistance, and international SAR insurance.

SPOT's Sat GPS Messenger is a standalone device that is fully functional without another GPS or smartphone. In 2010, the second generation satellite messenger hit the market. It is 30 percent smaller than the original and has a smarter SOS button and stronger GPS. (Now it's about the size of a PLB.)

The SPOT Connect uses Bluetooth technology to wirelessly pair with a smartphone or with Delorme's PN-60 GPS, which allows it to perform all of the functions of the Sat GPS Messenger plus send short texts and e-mails (41 characters max) for an extra fee. The Connect costs $150 plus the $100 annual basic plan. You also pay $0.50 per text or another annual fee for a bundle: 100 messages for $30 or 500 for $50. So now you can send your buddies back home a few short one-way texts from inside your tent at base camp on Gannet Peak.

One of the downsides of SPOT products is that Globalstar's satellite constellation does not currently cover the whole planet because many of their first-generation satellites have passed their life expectancies and are being retired. Today SPOT products will not work in the polar regions, most of India (where they are outlawed for security reasons), and parts of Africa. Globalstar is currently launching its second-generation satellite constellation, which should remedy that problem when it becomes operational sometime in the next few years.

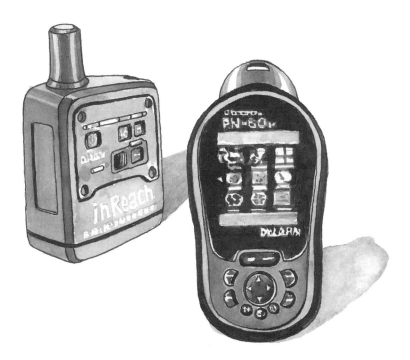

Delorme's PN-60w and inReach pair to allow two-way sattelite texting without a phone.

Delorme has been making maps since 1976 and has had a number of breakthroughs in GPS and map software technology over the years. After partnering with SPOT on the PN-60/SPOT Connect project, Delorme brought its own satellite communicator to the market in 2011. Delorme's first generation inReach ($250) is larger, heavier, and more expensive than either the SPOT Connect or the Sat GPS Messenger, and unlike the Connect, it can only pair with Android smartphones.

The Delorme inReach is not perfect, but it has two advantages over SPOT: it can operate either by pairing with a smartphone or PN-60 GPS (or it can perform basic functions as a standalone unit), and when paired with a smartphone or tablet, it allows you to receive as well as send texts. The ability for two-way communications means that you get message delivery confirmation and that emergency personnel have the opportunity to ask you followup questions about your location or the nature of the emergency. In addition to the price of the gadget, Delorme requires a $12 activation fee plus subscription to one of three plans: $10 per month (10 texts + unlimited SOS), $25 per month (40 texts, SOS, and tracking), or $50 per month (120 texts, SOS, tracking). All plans require a yearlong commitment, but you can switch between them at any time. Before you pay $50 per month, however, you might look in to renting a sat phone for the month you need it.

Delorme's inReach, in contrast to SPOT's devices, uses the Iridium satellite constellation, which currently has over 70 satellites in orbit and covers the planet.

Searching for a Lost Person

You can avoid having to search for a lost person by having the group agree that you will all stay within sight while you are moving. Clear camp boundaries and a designated general area

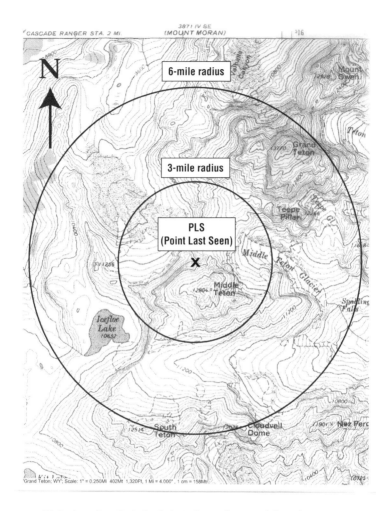

"Point Last Seen" circles help to focus the search for a lost person.

for bathroom use make it less likely that someone will wander too far from camp and get lost. If, however, someone from your group gets separated, use the following steps to make locating them easier.

Immediately give a few quick shouts and pause to listen for a response. Often, that's all it takes to locate someone nearby. If you get no response, mark the spot on the map where the person or group was last seen—the Point Last Seen (PLS). If the PLS is close (less than a quarter mile), head back right away to that spot, yelling or whistling every minute or so. Otherwise, draw two circles, one with a 3-mile radius around the PLS, another with a 6-mile radius. Half of all lost people are found within the first circle; a full 90 percent are found within the second. Focus your efforts within the first circle, and then the second one, keeping in mind these suggestions:

- Set up an area of confinement that boxes in the lost person by leaving notes, sleeping bags, or other signals in likely traffic areas like trail intersections and trailheads. Confine quickly and farther than you suspect the lost person may have gone.
- Determine the urgency of the situation by considering the lost person's age, mental state, wilderness skill level, clothing, food, gear, special medical concerns, weather, and terrain, as well as your own intuition.
- Identify likely areas the separated person might be and mark those on the map as well. Could they be looking for water? Trying to photograph something? Fishing? Did they make a wrong turn at a recent trail intersection?
- In an area where an accident is possible (places with steep rocks, river crossings, or other hazards), search potential accident sites first.
- Look downhill. Rarely do lost people stray uphill. Often, they simply keep descending when they are unsure where to go.
- If you have a large group, break into search teams and set specific meeting times and locations for reuniting. Send one team to the PLS and the rest to other likely areas.
- Have teams travel light and look for clues as well as the missing person.

- Don't search at night unless there is a true emergency. It is very strenuous and much less efficient.

You may use the method of drawing a circle to help you locate yourself if you become lost. Instead of the PLS, draw a circle around your last known point. How long have you traveled since you were there? The distance you can travel in that time should be the radius of your circle. Have you been going uphill or downhill? In one continuous direction or meandering a bit? What land features can you see that match those in the circle?

In North America, if you are long enough overdue, a search-and-rescue team will eventually be activated to locate your group. Often searches are conducted by both ground and air. An air search is likely if the weather permits—planes and helicopters will not fly in bad weather, and they generally will not fly at night either.

If you are resigned to sitting still and waiting to be rescued, here are some things you should know:

- Big searches in wilderness areas can take days. You will need food, water, and shelter if you are sitting and waiting. Stay organized and plan how you will conserve resources and stay alive during this period.
- You should camp in a visible area—the more open, the better. Try to get to a spot that is easily seen from above.
- Large, smoky fires are visible from great distances. Build one and keep it going. But don't make a bad problem worse by letting it get out of control. Make it visible, but keep it controlled by building it out in the open and away from trees.
- Carry signal mirrors and know how to use them before you need them in an emergency. Get out in the open and have them ready to use before you hear air traffic. SAR pilots say signal mirrors are the single most effective visual aid for identifying lost parties on the ground.

- Geometric patterns are often visible from the air. Triangles, squares, or circles made with rocks, branches, dirt, or extra gear may help. Brightly colored clothing and gear will also help to get you noticed—blues and reds are the most likely to get a pilot's attention.

Conclusion

Knowing how to take care of yourself and avoid getting lost is far more important than what gadgets you happen to have in your pack. Minimize the consequences of getting lost while you are learning to navigate by keeping your trips short and visiting areas where weather, large predators, and dangerous terrain cannot become life-threatening. Become comfortable navigating with map and compass without the aid of landmarks before heading out on a long off-trail trek.

Until you are an expert, don't consider traveling deep in the backcountry alone. Even then, you should be keenly aware of the risks you are taking by being alone. Once you have mastered foundational navigation skills, you can travel in more challenging environments and conditions.

Remember that if you activate an emergency beacon, you are asking people (oftentimes volunteers) to drop what they are doing and put themselves at risk for you. Before you press that button or make that phone call, be sure their risk is worth your emergency.

CHAPTER 8

DIGITAL MAPS, SMARTPHONE APPS, AND PORTABLE POWER

If you were to go out and buy all of the paper USGS maps for the state of Colorado, you would need to buy several hundred maps, at about $15 per map. For Alaska, you would need nearly one thousand. You might need an extra room in your house just to store all your new maps! One alternative is digital map software. With free maps available online and a variety of quality map programs available for less than $100, going digital is cheaper and easier.

Thanks to the newest generation of tablets, smartphones, and handheld GPS units, you now have the remarkable ability to see your exact location displayed on a digital topographic map in real time. This means that you can hold a gadget in your hands and watch your location on a digital map change as you move around on the ground. For younger readers who may have grown up with a touchscreen GPS in the family car, this may not seem like an innovation. But it is indeed, and it is changing the way people are interacting with wildlands. Like most things computer-related, handheld navigation technology is not just evolving, it is evolving at an ever-increasing rate. You can see your location on a topo-enhanced 3-D image of the area where you are standing or sight a distant peak on the horizon by holding your smartphone vertically and see the name of the the peak superimposed on the real-time video image on the screen. Imagine trying to explain this to your great-grandfather. This newer technology makes it easy to check your location and hard to get truly lost. Unfortunately, it also requires much more battery power than backpackers have ever carried with them in the past.

Map software does more than just provide electronic versions of paper maps. It also allows you to seamlessly connect and customize maps, plot routes, zoom in and out, find topographic features, create elevation profiles, upload and download GPS waypoints, and print your own custom maps to carry into the field with you.

Doing all of the above requires wading through some fairly serious computer terrain. If you are not computer savvy, this option isn't for you, and that's fine. For successful navigation,

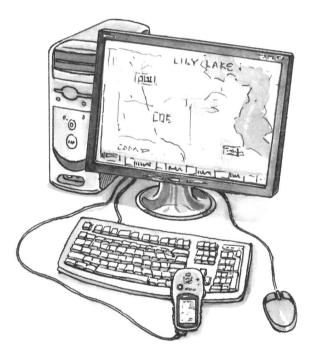

Hooking up your GPS to a computer allows you to download maps, back up data, and more.

digital mapping is not a must, just an option you may or may not choose to have in your navigation toolbox. The greatest feats of land-based exploration in world history have had nothing to do with electronics. Do not feel like you won't be a competent navigator unless you rush out and buy the gizmos mentioned here. But if the digital world is your thing, this chapter will point you toward some exciting new ways to increase your navigation speed and accuracy.

Even if you are computer-literate, you may still choose NOT to bring current communication technology with you in to the field. Lugging a digital arsenal of smartphone, GPS, tablet computer, and so forth into the wilderness can seriously detract from an otherwise completely self-reliant trip. If your wilderness experience involves routinely checking e-mails, texting, and updating your social network profile pic, you need to ask yourself why you even left home. A lot can be learned by being immersed in an environment that is untouched and uncontrolled by humankind. (In fact, a lot can be learned by being lost in the wilderness and having to find your way out on your own.) Are you an expedition leader who really needs communication technology in case a group member becomes ill or injured and needs to be evacuated? Or are you a weekend warrior who is bringing the distractions of the modern world into the one place you could visit to get away from all that? Thinking about your or your group's reasons for wilderness travel will help you decide what to take and what not to take.

Also keep in mind that the potential combinations of electronic navigation gadgets one might choose to carry are becoming mind-boggling even for the technophiles. What you choose to add to your digital arsenal may depend more on the size of your bank account and your current operating system than on your reasons for traveling in the wilderness.

Once again, a simple paper map, a magnetic compass, and your brain can get you where you need to go in most environ-

Electronic gadgets can be helpful navigation tools, but don't overdo it.

ments on earth. Never undertrain the computer between your ears. Electronics can enhance your navigation skills, but should not be used to bypass developing those skills in the first place. Learn to navigate with map and compass *first*. To do otherwise is to bet your life that your batteries won't run out and leave you stranded. If you have been going out and successfully completing the exercises at the end of each chapter of this book, then you're ready to start thinking about digital maps and the gadgetry that makes them work.

Map Software

There are essentially three kinds of topo-map software available to recreational users: GPS manufacturer software, off-the-shelf map software, and web-based map software. All three can be used to plan a route on your computer and print customized maps. You can draw in the best route, mark campsites or points of interest, and get coordinates. By simply moving your cursor across the computer screen, you can find the coordinates of any location on the map in UTM, latitude/longitude, or virtually any other coordinate system. Most map software now features elevation profiles, hill shading, satellite imagery, and three-dimensional views. Some also allow you to search by feature name, place name, or coordinates, or to overlay symbols and text for marking a point on the map. Switching from satellite images to topo lines, particularly in an area you know well, can help you better understand how topo lines take their shape.

The system requirements for running most digital map software has become less expensive and much less complicated over the last five years. If your computer (Mac or PC) is less than three years old, you probably have all the processing power and memory you need to run most map software packages. Nonetheless, you should double-check that your computer's operating system and processor meet the requirements of any software you are thinking of purchasing.

Most GPS handhelds today come preloaded with topo maps for the country in which they are sold, meaning you don't need to spend time and energy locating and downloading the particular map you need for a trip. If you are purchasing a handheld, it makes sense to buy one with preloaded maps, which tend to function more seamlessly than standalone or online maps. However, many GPS units today are designed to work directly with Google Earth.

A decade ago, map software for wilderness navigation was used only by the military, a few professionals, and a handful of dedicated recreationists. Since 2005, almost anyone with a high-speed Internet connection and newer laptop has been able to use outstanding map software free of charge thanks to Google. Google now reports that Google Earth has been downloaded more than a billion times. If you are not one of those billion, you owe it to yourself to try the free download even if you have no interest in digital maps. Nothing beats being in the field and comparing the land features you are seeing to the map you are holding in your hands, but the ability to zoom in and out and scroll through terrain like Superman gives you a rough understanding of the scale and complexity of any wilderness terrain on the planet before you even set foot on the ground. That understanding will only enhance your ability to accurately plan and follow wilderness routes. For the majority of recreationists, Google Earth is the only map software they will ever need. And it's free.

National Geographic and Delorme both sell quality off-the-shelf map software that doesn't require an Internet connection to work well. Storing digital maps, unlike simply running a mapping program, uses a lot of storage space. If you are planning to store a lot of digital maps and have an older computer, consider using a CD-ROM burner to store maps on CDs, purchasing an external hard drive for storage, or storing them somewhere in the cloud (using an online storage service).

If you will be printing maps from your own computer, you'll also want a good color printer. Black-and-white copies of topos are confusing and often difficult to use. Before you commit to printing all your own maps, remember that they will only ever be as large as your printer will allow. Unless you spend thousands of dollars on a five-foot-long standing map printer or take a lot of time taping pages together, your maps will never be the size of standard USGS quads. Consider printing maps in a couple of different scales of the area you will be visiting.

Smartphone vs. Smart-GPS

By connecting a GPS to your computer, you can upload or download waypoints, tracks, routes, or map data. This means that you can plan routes on your computer and then upload them to your GPS. It also gives you the ability to leave your GPS set to track while you are out and then overlay your tracks onto a digital map when you get back home. You can then compare your map and compass-based location estimates with the GPS data—another great way to build your terrain association skills. Remember, however, that some older GPS units do not display maps. If your GPS only has a basic display, you won't be able to view data on a topo map image until you upload those tracks to a computer that has compatible software or Internet access.

The alternative to standalone GPS handhelds with a map display is a smartphone or tablet computer with GPS capability. Most smartphones sold since 2010 have GPS hardware built in. Smartphones and tablets in the wilderness, however, still present other major challenges:

1. They must be charged regularly. This requires that you lug along some kind of portable power (see page 166 for a full discussion of portable power).
2. They are more fragile than GPS handhelds and require specialized cases. Lifeproof is among the companies that make a variety of cases with clear plastic windows that allow use of the touchscreen. Some tablet cases allow you

to slip your hand through a strap in the back to easily monitor the larger screen with one hand while in the field.

3. Some navigation apps will not work without Wi-Fi or cellular signal. Make sure that if you are using a smartphone app to access maps, you download all the maps you'll need into your device before you travel out of range.

When I wrote the first edition of this book back in 2004, smartphones (more commonly called Portable Digital Assistants or PDAs at that time) had these advantages over handheld GPS units:

• The touchscreen or stylus made them easier to use than some tiny GPS buttons.

• Larger, high-resolution, color screens made it easier to read digital maps.

• GPS users were limited to maps made by the GPS manufacturer.

Garmin recognized all of this and developed several GPS models that look and act like smartphones with dedicated navigation apps. Their Oregon, Montana, and Dakota series handhelds feature touchscreens, cameras, barometric altimeters, preloaded topo maps, and wireless data sharing. Meanwhile, Delorme designed its Earthmate PN-60w to wirelessly interact with satellite communicators to allow two-way texting.

Unfortunately, many of these smart-GPS models also cost as much or more than a smartphone. So if you already own a smartphone, why buy one of these? Most GPS units provide longer battery life while in navigation mode (four to twenty-four hours) than smartphones running navigation apps (one to four hours). And you can replace batteries in GPS handhelds in the field. So if you don't already own a smartphone or you don't want to mess with portable power and daily recharging, a smart-GPS unit might be the gadget of choice for you.

Delorme and Garmin make GPS units with smartphone features.

Smartphone Apps as Wilderness Navigation Tools

There are many reasons aside from navigation or emergency communication that someone might want to carry a tablet or smartphone into the wilderness. For example, less than a decade ago, I went on several 30-day NOLS expeditions in the North Cascades where twelve of us carried a combined weight of over 40 pounds in books and another 10 pounds in cameras. With a growing number of natural history applications for tablets and smartphones designed for field use (e.g., Audubon Guides) carrying a few tablets and a solar recharger is starting to look inviting. But whatever your reasons for owning a tablet or smartphone, you need to understand a few key things about what they can and cannot do to assist you with wilderness navigation.

A tablet computer with GPS hardware can process GPS data and display your location on a screen that is larger than those found on most GPS handhelds. The large touchscreen and high resolution makes it simple to zoom in on otherwise tough-to-read areas of the map. In effect, tablet-size screens make digital map reading in the field much easier and more effective than reading paper maps. Tablets won't blow away in a light breeze and make it simple to look at those border areas where you need to hold four maps together to see where you are headed.

The tradeoffs, however, are also significant—the potential to detrain our brains for terrain association and the unending need for recharging, which we'll discuss below, are the two big ones. They also have the potential for electromagnetic interference (near power lines for example), which messes with the accuracy of the device's digital compass. Touchscreens don't work well with gloves. And before you break in to your piggy bank to buy an iPad for your big trip to the Karakorum, you should know that Apple's website lists 10,000 feet (3000 meters) as the max operating altitude for both iPhone and iPad. Worse, the operating temperature is listed between 32°F (0C) and 95°F (35°C) and the non-operating temperature is between -4°F (-20°C) and 113°F (45°C). You can keep your iPad or iPhone inside your layers or otherwise insulated from extreme temps, but that can be tedious and requires notable diligence. Positive early anecdotal evidence among American mountaineers suggests that iPhones function well above 10,000 feet if they are kept warm and dry. The jury is still out on whether the instrumentation and larger glass touchscreens on the tablets can survive at higher altitudes, but I suggest leaving them at base camp for now.

Depending on the brand and model of your device, the amount of navigation-related hardware sensors built in is baffling. In addition to the digital compass, accelerometer, and integrated GPS (of iPhone 3G and later), some smartphones now have a 3-axis gyroscope (such as iPhone 4 and later). Without diving too deeply into the physics behind this technology, the gyroscope can combine data with the accelerometer to provide the gadget with awareness of its speed, distance, and directionality in three-dimensional space. A few years ago, this kind of technology could only be found on satellites, planes, and rockets.

Applications (apps) are computer software that allow you to use the data from the hardware stuffed into these tiny gadgets. The most powerful apps are able to combine data from all of this hardware with map data to provide you with stunningly accurate and easy-to-understand navigation information.

If you go searching for GPS apps on the Internet, most of what you will stumble across are apps based on street atlases for road use. Some apps are server-based—they require an Internet connection to constantly download the appropriate map as you travel. These usually have a subscription fee you'll need to pay in addition to buying the app. Avoid them. Your one-time fee should include a preloaded database of maps. Make sure your device and navigation apps will store and display topographic maps without an Internet connection. Certain apps may not work with your cellular service provider. For example, some AT&T apps don't work with Verizon and vice versa. Many apps will only work with the latest operating system. And of course, apps designed for Android phones and apps designed for iPhones are not interchangeable. Check before you download.

Like most smartphone apps, wilderness navigation apps seem to be multiplying like rabbits. They tend to fall into three categories: simple map databases, GPS features, and augmented reality (AR), the newest category. Here are a few of my favorites:

- MAPLETS ($3). iPhone and iPad only. This map database app allows you to select and download from a library of 5,000 maps. While a few popular topos are included, the database features a much wider variety of street, trail, and park maps.

- MAPRIKA (free). iPhone, iPad, and Android. The brilliance of this app is that it not only allows you to download and store many types of maps on your device for free, it also uses GPS to show you your tracks and location on those 2,000 maps. So you can see your current location on maps of college campuses, mountain bike trails, or ski resorts.
- GPS STATUS (free). iPhone, iPad, and Android. This basic diagnostic tool allows you to see which satellites the GPS in your device is picking up. This tells you how accurate your position fix is (say, within 10 meters). Many GPS apps also have this feature built in.
- TRAIL MAPS BY NATIONAL GEOGRAPHIC ($3). iPhone and iPad only. This is a reliable USGS topo-map database of the entire United States, which also allows standard GPS functions like tracking, waypoints, speed, elevation profiles, distance to destination, and heading. Strangely, it does not specifically highlight particular trails, despite the app name.
- ALLTRAILS (free). iPhone, iPad, and Android. This topo-map database is based on the free OpenCycle and OpenStreet map database. While the maps don't have quite the detail as the USGS quads, they do have accurate contours. And the app allows for all of the same GPS functions listed above.
- COMPASS PRO ($1). iPhone and iPad only. There are tons of compass apps out there. This one beats them all with a unique real-time floating azimuth effect, multiple needle displays that show both true and magnetic headings, levels, GPS coordinates (with accuracy range), elevation (with accuracy range)—all on one easy-to-read screen. It also has a Google map view of your heading for times when you have an Internet connection.

Augmented Reality Navigation Apps

The future of electronically assisted wilderness navigation lies in a user interface known as augmented reality (AR). Augmented reality is viewing the real physical world through a live camera image that adds computer-generated sensory input such as position, heading, speed, distance to destination, or points of interest. AR is what the world looks like from the Terminator's perspective; that is to say, you can see the world around you, but you also have additional information appearing in your field of view.

The gaming industry is rapidly developing AR. Ski goggles with integrated GPS data (Zeal Transcend) are already on the market. Google and Oakley, among others, are currently racing to be the first to bring wearable AR glasses to the masses.

What makes the AR navigation experience so unique is not only the continuous navigation data, but also the way the data is presented. It feels as if you can see your destination or point of interest directly through whatever buildings or land features might be in the way. This will change the way land navigation is done, particularly in low visibility emergency situations. If you can "see" your destination through a thick forest of trees by merely panning around with your phone, you can hardly get lost (at least until the batteries run out, which may not be long).

The first generation of AR apps for navigation are now available—Theodolite Pro ($5) and Spyglass ($4).

A traditional theodolite is an optical instrument that measures vertical and horizontal angles for surveying, meteorology, and navigation. Manual theodolites that use azimuth rings, levels, and telescopes on a tripod have been in use since the 1700s, but this version is a bit more advanced, to say the least. At first glance, Theodolite Pro looks like a screen you might see in the cockpit of a 747. You hold your smartphone up as if you are taking a picture horizontally. As you look more closely at the onscreen features, you notice that within your camera screen view you can also see the GPS position, altitude, current time, and compass bearing. You can easily measure the angle of a slope in the distance using the horizon angle, or a slope directly above you using the elevation angle. At the touch of the screen, you can change screen colors to preserve night vision or zoom up to 4X.

Still not impressed? Tapping the center of the screen brings up an optical rangefinder. If you know the height of the object you are sighting (a target, for example), the rangefinder can tell you the distance to that object. You can also estimate the height of a distant object if you know the distance to it. Because it knows your coordinates and sighting angles, the app can use triangulation to tell you the distance to any unknown point that you can sight from two different and relatively distant locations. You can also take geo-tagged photos and screenshots and view your current position on Google maps.

Spyglass is a newer and slightly less intimidating but equally fascinating AR navigation app. It includes almost all of the same features as Theodolite Pro (including sextant, optical rangefinder, gyrocompass, and inclinometer) but in a different format. Spyglass also allows you to hold your device as if taking a photo either vertically or horizontally. A translucent onscreen azimuth ring rotates as you pan left or right to give you your heading. You can zoom in and out using pinch gestures. Best of all, when you simply lower the device so the screen is parallel to the ground, it instantly switches to an overhead map view showing your current location relative to waypoints and points of interest. From the overhead view, you can mark a waypoint by tapping the screen and then raise your device and see the virtual waypoint as you pan left to right—an astoundingly intuitive and accurate way to mark waypoints and follow a bearing in any terrain or visibility conditions. As a bonus, the app also allows you to see celestial features as if looking through the earth. If you already own a newer smartphone and are learning to navigate in the wilderness, this app will help.

There are countless apps that will perform single navigation functions like provide a digital compass display, give your elevation, or track your mountain bike ride. But why clutter your device with so many apps when you really just need a few that can serve all of those key functions? Select a few apps you like, practice using them regularly, and get to know them well before you really need them.

Now for the bad news . . . what makes these navigation apps do so many interesting things is their ability to engage and combine all of the phone's hardware at once. That same ability kills the phone's batteries. The camera and GPS are huge drains and require a recharge after just two to three hours of continuous use (if you are lucky). GPS apps kill batteries even while they are running in the background. You can switch to airplane mode, but that disables the GPS as well as the Bluetooth, cellular, and Wi-Fi. So when and how you decide to use these powerful new tools is critical. On expeditions, the smart move is to simply save the batteries for emergency use, such as traveling at night or in a blizzard. Even then, you will need a recharge if you plan to use the device the next day. If you are using the device for anything other than navigation or communication and you are in an area with weak or no cell signal, keep it powered off or in airplane mode. Constantly searching for a cell signal (even while driving to the trailhead) will kill the batteries as quickly as having the camera or GPS running. Understanding how to conserve battery power in your device is as important as understanding how to use it for navigation.

If you plan to use navigation apps with a smartphone or tablet, consider also buying a case that provides additional battery power as well as protection from the weather. Mophie makes several of these that double your battery life for both Apple and Android phones and tablets.

Portable Power for the Wilderness

Think of portable power hardware as having two parts—a solar panel to capture energy and a battery pack to store the energy and move it to your device. A growing variety of both solar panels and battery packs include those that combine panel and battery pack into one unit (Joos, Solio Bolt, and Brunton Restore) and solar panels that connect directly to your device without a battery pack—but for multiday trips away from grid-based power sources, you will want both a solar panel and a battery pack of some kind. The panel puts energy into the battery pack during the day, and the pack stores the energy so that it can charge your device at night or whenever you are not using it. While you can connect the panels directly to your device, they must be in direct sun and the batteries take much longer to charge than if you use a battery pack.

Portable solar panels (or photovoltaic panels, also known as PVs) come in three different types: Monocrystalline, polycrystalline, and CIGS panels. Monocrystalline panels, which are black, tend to be slightly more efficient per square inch than polycrystalline panels, which have an iridescent color similar to fish scales. CIGS panels are about half as efficient as both types of crystalline panels, but they are lighter weight, more durable, and flexible. So if you tend to be rough on your gear, consider CIGS. The downside of CIGS is that while it is lighter per square inch than crystalline panels, you will need around twice as much area to get the same charging rate as crystalline.

In general, more and larger panels mean faster power collection. Key questions to ask are how much does the whole kit weigh, how long does it take to charge, what is the storage capacity of the battery, and how fast can it recharge your device.

Portable solar power for backpacking is still in its infancy, but there are several great products already on the market that work far better than what was available just three years ago. The best setups I have field-tested for wilderness backpacking are from Brunton, Goal Zero, and Joos.

PORTABLE POWER OPTIONS FOR SMARTPHONES AND TABLETS

- Joos Orange ($150). Monocrystalline panel with integrated battery, weighs 24 ounces, stores 20 watt hours/5400mAh, output of 1000A/5V.
- Brunton-Resync with Solaris 4 Panel ($428). Combined weight is 16.3 ounces, stores 9000mA, output of 2100mA/5V, CIGS panel.
- Goal Zero-Guide 10 Plus Adventure Kit ($160). Weighs 16 ounces, stores 10 watt hours, output of 1A/5V (5 watts), monocrystalline panel.

The Joos Orange provides the most power dollar for dollar, but at 24 ounces, it is quite heavy for backpacking. About the size and weight of a hardback college textbook, it has an efficient integrated battery. It is also the simplest setup to use and can be cable-locked to a tree in a busy campground while you are away.

Brunton offers a wide variety of panels and batteries depending on your needs. For smartphone- or tablet-supported backpacking, the Resync battery pack with the Solaris 4 USB solar panel seems like the best combination from Brunton. The Brunton panels are the most durable and weatherproof and are also notably lighter than the Joos Orange. However, it is hard to justify the $428 price tag in comparison to Goal Zero's Guide 10 Plus Adventure Kit.

The Guide 10 Plus kit is not only the lightest setup but also includes AA or AAA rechargeable batteries, which can power

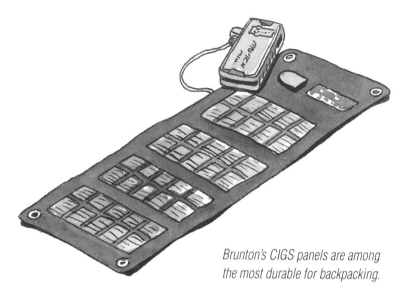

*Brunton's CIGS panels are among
the most durable for backpacking.*

other devices. So if you plan to use rechargeables for headlamps, handheld GPS, or other electronics, Goal Zero is the best option. For the money, weight, and utility, Goal Zero is the way to go.

Brunton and Goal Zero both offer headlamps that charge directly through their portable power products. But with the Goal Zero Guide 10 kit, you could use any AA or AAA battery powered headlamp.

It is tempting to rig a panel to your backpack in an attempt to trickle-charge your device as you hike. In fact, there are already a few book-bag backpacks with built-in panels. Unfortunately, the panel technology is not quite good enough yet for this to be very effective for wilderness backpacking. As you are hiking, the changing angle of the sun makes it hard for the panels to get a significant charge. You have to angle the panels directly at the sun to maximize energy capture, which means that for now, you are probably only going to be charging your battery in camp. For most folks, a lowly 10 percent net charge

iPhones charge more efficiently from a battery pack than directly from a panel.

over five hours of hiking in the mountains is probably not worth the hassle of attaching panels to the backpack.

Use rechargeable batteries when you can. It is the environmentally smart thing to do, and it will save you some dollars in the long run. While no rechargeables can hold a single charge as long as a regular disposable alkaline, nickel metal hybrides (NiMH) stay charged the longest and can be used up to one thousand times. Older nickel cadmium (NiCad) batteries don't hold a charge for long and are not worth your money. Rechargeable alkalines are cheaper than NiMH, but won't stay charged as long and need to be replaced more often.

Smartphone cases, such as those from Lifeproof, make your phone waterproof, dustproof, and shockproof.

If recharging is not an option or you will be in extreme cold, take disposable lithium batteries. While they are considerably more expensive, lithiums are lighter and have the longest single charge of any battery. Lithium-ions are convenient around town and are great for short trips. If you will be in the backcountry for an extended period of time, be sure that you know how long your device will stay charged. Without battery power, you'll be carrying around an expensive, fragile brick for the rest of your trip.

If you intend to bring a smartphone into the wilderness for navigation use, you should strongly consider a supplemental battery pack like Mophie's Juice Pack Pro. The Juice Pack Pro is a rain-, shock-, and dust-proof case with a built-in battery. The extra battery extends the phone's battery life by 150 percent. While it also nearly doubles the phone's thickness and weight, that extra power is well worth it. The Juice Pack Pro worked seamlessly with the portable power options described above in field tests. For a tough case option without a battery, try the low-profile smartphone cases from Lifeproof.

A final commonsense note on battery-powered navigation gadgets: while following the magic GPS arrow can be very handy, you may have a tough time getting up the cliffs and through the crevasse fields it is pointing you toward—your map software won't do the routefinding, river-crossing, or crevasse rescue for you. Remember that just because the arrow points you toward the most direct route doesn't mean it's the best route. Stories of drivers following a GPS route down an obscure dirt road only to become stuck in a blizzard are adding up. Don't let your smartphone or GPS get you into terrain you don't have the proper skills for.

CHAPTER 9 | COMPETITIVE NAVIGATION

Once you've been in the field developing your basic navigation skills, it is time to look at advanced ways to apply those
skills and further boost your learning. This section gives you
some background and offers tips and suggestions for competitive navigation.

Unless you are a wilderness instructor or are in the military,
you will have to seek out ways on your own to test and improve
your navigation skills. Whether you are competitive by nature or
just want to sharpen your eye for maps, there are a number of
sporting events that may suit your navigation needs. Many of
these competitions are designed specifically for those who are
relatively new to backcountry travel. Competitions needn't be
about winning ribbons or medals. Think of the events mentioned here as an organized way for you to compete against
yourself and measure your improvement. They are a fantastic
opportunity to meet folks with similar interests, learn from the
experts, see what is possible, and practice in a more controlled
environment. Where else can you run through woods at night
and get occasional hot meals, meet with support crews, and
have medics standing by to help in case of an emergency?

There are three navigation-based sports to consider depending on your time and interests: orienteering, rogaining, and
adventure racing. If you are the gung-ho type and want to try all
three, take them in that order. An ideal progression would be to

attend some orienteering meets before attempting a rogaine, and trying a 24-hour rogaine or two before navigating a multi-day adventure race.

Your goal for your first orienteering meet or rogaine might simply be to get off the start line. Finishing one of these events is quite an accomplishment. You should "race to finish" for several races before thinking about improving your placement against others. Your first year, in fact, should not be focused on what place you finish, but on learning, meeting people, and having fun.

Orienteering

Orienteering is the sport of cross-country navigation with map and compass. After beginning as a Scandinavian military exercise in the late nineteenth century, it was popularized by the Swedish in Europe and made its debut in the United States in the 1940s. Today, there are orienteering clubs across the world linked together through the International Orienteering Federation (IOF) and the United States Orienteering Federation (USOF).

Orienteering meets typically feature a number of courses set up for various skill levels. Beginner courses may only be a mile long, while expert courses can be more than ten miles. Individuals compete by hiking and running through a series of "control points" that are marked by flags. Competitors start off at different times, following a marked map and description sheet to each point, where there is a special punch to mark your control card and show that you were there. Selecting the best route between controls is the primary challenge of the sport. The fastest time through the course with the control card punched correctly wins.

Orienteering maps are usually 1:10,000 scale and have a lot more detail than typical topo maps. They are set to magnetic north to remove declination confusion. Many maps will also include details on the vegetation density to help you plan your route. Different colors are often used for this. For example, yellow may indicate open land, white may mean a forested area that is still runnable, and dark green may indicate terrain that is very thick or impassable. First-time competitors need to pay careful attention to the legend on their map and expect some differences from standard topos.

Many competitors become attracted to the sport because it demands mental as well as physical endurance. The best orienteers are excellent map-readers who can run, not excellent runners still learning to read a map—how fast you run doesn't matter much when you are running in the wrong direction. Experienced, competitive orienteers do train by running long distances on- and off-trail. As a beginner, however, you should focus primarily on sharpening your map-reading skills. With the excitement of a meet, your speed will pick up automatically.

Here are a few tips for orienteering:

- Don't forget to warm up before the start. (10 to 15 minutes of light jogging helps.)
- Stay hydrated and well-fed before, during, and after the meet.
- Choose the easiest-to-follow route between controls for your first few meets.
- Start on the easier (white or yellow) courses.
- Try counting paces as described in chapter 4. Get to know your speed and stride length in different kinds of terrain. Have a system for counting paces by the hundred, and know how many of your paces are in a mile.
- Don't follow other competitors. It's poor etiquette, and besides, they may not be headed the right way.

- Wear light pants or gaiters to protect your legs from brush on the advanced courses.

As orienteering—or simply "O"—meets have grown in popularity over the last ten years, so have the variety of formats. Today, there are special orienteering meets for mountain bikers (Bike-O) and cross-country skiers (Ski-O). Some meets are held at night (Night-O) to challenge nighttime navigation skills like compass use and pace counting.

To learn more about orienteering meets near you, visit the websites of the International Orienteering Federation (www.orienteering.org) and the US Orienteering Federation (www.us.orienteering.org). Local orienteering clubs also usually have websites and e-mail lists with calendars to keep you posted on upcoming events.

Rogaining

ROGAINE is an acronym for "Rugged Outdoor Group Activity Involving Navigation and Endurance." The sport of rogaining was born in Australia in the mid-1970s. It differs from classic point-to-point orienteering in several critical ways: rogaines are team events (two to five people on a team), they last much longer (three to twenty-four hours), and the controls—known as checkpoints—have different point values and can be visited in any order.

Because the checkpoints are spread out over longer distances, most rogaines use smaller-scale (1:24,000 or 1:50,000) maps. A central base camp is set up throughout the race where teams can eat, rest, or plan their next moves. Because teams can travel at their own pace and go any distance they choose, virtually anyone of any age can participate.

Teamwork and team strategy play a major role in rogaining. As with adventure racing, team members must work together to set the best pace, plan their route, and support each other through the course. A rogaining course is planned so that no team can reach all of the checkpoints in the allotted time. Teams are forced to choose which checkpoints to head for. Whether you choose to aim for more distant or harder-to-find checkpoints with higher point values, and whether you save the harder checkpoints for daytime hours and focus on easier ones at night, is up to your team. The team also has to choose whether to search through the night or get a few hours of sleep. The clock, however, keeps ticking.

One unique feature of rogaines is that everyone finishes at the same time, unlike other traditional races, where the stragglers arrive as the leaders have just packed up or hit the showers. This allows all skill levels to mingle and is particularly nice for those newer to the sport.

Orienteering clubs and meets are a great place to meet future teammates for a rogaine, and most orienteering clubs will have rogaines on their calendar. Another source for rogaines near you is the International Rogaining Federation (IRF) at www.rogaining.com.

Some tips for rogaining:

- Know your teammate(s). Train together, discuss your goals, and communicate, communicate, communicate.
- Start with a few shorter races (less than 12 hours) before tackling a day-long pain-fest.
- Consider sleeping for several hours during your first 24-hour race. Plan your sleep strategy with your teammate(s).
- Eat the same foods and use the same clothing and gear during the race that you use while training.
- Train at night and in bad weather.

Adventure Racing

Adventure racing is team, multisport, endurance racing that takes place predominantly in backcountry settings. The standard components of an adventure race are mountain biking, paddling, off-trail running or hiking, and ascending or descending fixed ropes. Depending on the location, some races also feature events like glacier mountaineering, canyoneering, open water swimming, kayaking, caving, horseback riding, diving, skydiving, or sailing. Races vary in length from several hours to several weeks and cover distances from 5 to 700 miles. They are typically nonstop events where the clock runs continuously and sleep management is a critical part of team strategy. However, there are a few multiday stage races that are structured more like the Tour de France. For most adventure races, navigation—whether by boat, bike, or foot—is a constant challenge.

In 1989, French journalist and adventurer Gerard Fusil launched the sport of adventure racing with the first annual Raid Gauloises (pronounced "raid gall-wahz"). The first Raid required coed teams of five to traverse the South Island of New Zealand together by foot, bicycle, and boat. The Raid was a huge success and was followed in 1995 by the Eco-Challenge Expedition Race, which popularized the sport in North America and around the world until its final race in 2002. New Zealand's Southern Traverse, China's Mild Seven Outdoor Quest, and the United States' own Primal Quest are similar in length (five to fifteen days). For the less masochistic, shorter outdoor obstacle course races like the Spartan Race series and the Tough Mudder Race series offer a similar flavor but without the navigation challenges of true adventure races. The shorter races (three hours to three days) have made adventure racing accessible to recreational athletes wanting to test their navigation skills and endurance; they also are more affordable and less the exclusive domain of marathoners, pro cyclists, and tri-athletes.

Some tips for adventure racing:

- Know your teammates before you race with them. Train together when you can. Be sure you all have the same goal. Are you racing to finish or to win? What if someone becomes injured? How much sleep will you need, and when will you take it? How will finances be split? Take the time to iron out all these details when the team is forming, not on the racecourse.

- Nothing will drain your energy and slow you down like serious disagreements during the race. Avoid them like the plague or you will wish you had. When navigation errors are made (and they will be), support the navigator by minimizing the impact of the error and focusing on getting back on track.

- Make sure every person on your team is at least minimally competent in each event of the race. Encourage everyone to be open and honest about personal skills, limits, and fears, both before and during the race. A tone of honest and open communication is critical and starts long before you reach the start line.

- Give some of your pack weight to your teammates when you are struggling, and take their weight when they are struggling. Vigilantly watch for ways to support each other. It is common to hear rogainers and adventure racers say that the team "is only as fast as the slowest person." Smart teams actually race faster than the slowest person could go on their own by encouraging each other and sharing weight.

- Don't waste time in transition (rest) areas. Have your gear organized, and have a time limit planned for every transition.

- Make sure each person has a role: team captain, lead navigator, timekeeper, health (food/hydration) monitor, and so forth.
- Have more than one competent navigator on your team. Who takes over when the primary navigator becomes ill? Who makes that decision? When?
- Train at night and in bad weather.

Afterword

Let's step past the technical skills and challenges involved in wilderness navigation today and look to the future. Two of the most pressing issues changing the way backcountry travel happens today are land access and technological advances. By looking ahead, we can plan more effectively.

Protecting Public Land Access

Whether you go to the backcountry to hike, fish, backpack, hunt, climb, run, bike, ride horses, boat, or just get away, you should be thinking about land access. The better you understand how the land you are traveling on is managed, the better you will be able to ensure that your access to those areas is not denied one day. Unless you own or have permission to travel on large areas of private land, public land access issues affect you. Talk to land management organizations like the US Forest Service, the Bureau of Land Management, and the National Park Service about issues that may threaten your access and what you can do to help. Public lands in North America and many other parts of the world face ongoing threats, from overdevelopment to overuse.

In areas near large population centers, we are loving our public lands to death. When we disrupt and pollute the natural state of public lands enough, land managers restrict or temporarily deny access so that those areas can recover. When you have a choice, choose the road less traveled and avoid crowded, highly impacted areas. Do your part by carefully following the Leave No Trace principles in the introduction to this book every time you visit the backcountry.

With the excitement of competitive events, it can be easy to overlook ecological impacts that you or your team may have on the area you are visiting. Be especially vigilant about following the Leave No Trace principles at these events. Land managers are appropriately concerned about the concentrated impacts that large groups can have on public lands. If you do decide to compete, race without a trace. If you host an event or are leading a group, you have a responsibility to make sure that group knows how to minimize their impacts.

Wilderness Navigation Technology

Love it or hate it, gadgets designed to make traveling in the wilderness easier will continue growing in variety and popularity. Navigation toys will keep getting lighter, tougher, more affordable, and more multifunctional.

Smartphones will continue to incorporate bigger screens that make them better tools for map reading and satellite capabilities that make emergency communication effective outside of cell phone tower range. As satellite capabilities become more common in smartphones, synergies between the Internet and electronic navigation tools will change wilderness travel. Having a solar-charged smartphone with full GPS capability, a library of topo maps, and satellite communication is already a reality. Soon it will be an all-in-one device. Augmented reality applications will continue to develop and one day allow smartphone users to identify any distant land feature visible on the phone's screen.

Technological advances, however, are only useful to the extent that they make it easier or provide more time for us to do the things we love. If getting there truly is half the fun, we have to be careful not to take the fun out of how we get there. We must also keep in mind why we go. For many of us, navigating by paper map and magnetic compass alone is an exciting and rewarding challenge. What a great feeling to push through three miles of tough jungle and arrive at that pristine waterfall you recognized on the map! How many times have wayward explorers discovered a spectacular cave or unknown canyon while bumbling desperately off-course?

Be clear with yourself about your reasons for heading into the wild. If you know why you are going and what's important about your trip, you can decide what technology, if any, is worth taking. Whatever your reasons for venturing into the backcountry, be safe and enjoy the journey!

A | Where to Find Maps

TOPOGRAPHIC MAPS
US Government Agencies
store.usgs.gov
    US Geological Survey Map Store
www.nps.gov
    National Park Service
www.fs.fed.us
    US Forest Service
www.blm.gov
    Bureau of Land Management

NATIONAL GEOGRAPHIC TRAILS
ILLUSTRATED PLASTIC MAPS
http://shop.nationalgeographic.com

ONLINE MAP RESOURCE
https://maps.google.com/

B | Websites

WILDERNESS AND NAVIGATION SKILL DEVELOPMENT

www.nols.edu
> Wilderness skills and leadership development worldwide

www.nols.edu/nolspro
> Custom skills seminars for groups on land navigation and leadership

www.nols.edu/wmi
> Wilderness first aid training, including WEMT, WFR, and WFA certifications

ORIENTEERING

www.orienteering.org
> International Orienteering Federation

www.us.orienteering.org
> US Orienteering Federation

ROGAINING

www.rogaining.com
> International Rogaining Federation

ADVENTURE RACING

www.sleepmonsters.com, www.rev3adventure.com, www.checkpointtracker.com, and www.usara.com
> News and race information

Suggested Reading

Burns, Bob and Mike. *Wilderness Navigation*, 2nd ed. The Mountaineers. 2004.

Cooper, Donald. *Fundamentals of Search and Rescue*. NASAR. Jones and Bartlett Publishers. 2005.

Eng, Ronald. *Mountaineering: Freedom of the Hills*, 8th ed. The Mountaineers. 2010.

Gookin, John et al. *NOLS Wilderness Educator Notebook*. The National Outdoor Leadership School. 2003.

Harvey, Mark. *NOLS Wilderness Guide*. Fireside, Simon & Schuster. 1999.

Letham, Lawrence and Alex. *GPS Made Easy*, 5th ed. The Mountaineers. 2008.

Mann, Don, and Karen Schaad. *The Complete Guide to Adventure Racing*. Hatherleigh Press. 2001.

McNamara, Joel. *GPS For Dummies*. Wiley Publishing, Inc. 2004.

O'Bannon, Allen, and Mike Clelland. *Allen & Mike's Really Cool Backpackin' Book*. The Globe Pequot Press. 2001.

Phillips, Neil and Rod. *Rogaining: Cross-Country Navigation*, 3rd ed. Outdoor Recreation in Australia. 2000.

Rey, H. A. *The Stars: A New Way To See Them*. Houghton Mifflin Company. 1997.

Tilton, Buck. *The Leave No Trace Master Educator Handbook*. The National Outdoor Leadership School, The Leave No Trace Center for Outdoor Ethics. 2003.

Index

ACR Cobham PLBs, 141–142
adventure racing, 172, 177–179, 184
altimeter-barometers, 38
altimeters, 91–99
apps for navigation, 159–166
attack points, 77
augmented reality (AR) apps, 163–165
azimuth ring, 34, 44

back bearings, 55–56
backstops, 76, 78
back tracking, 137
back-tracking GPS feature, 125–126
barometric altimeters, 92–96
bar scale, 9
base plate (compass), 34
base-plate compasses, 37–38
batteries, 93, 129, 143, 158, 165–171
bearing(s)
    following, 47–52
    locating position using, 58–60, 137–138
    skills practice, 60–65
    taking and plotting, 52–58
benchmarks (BM), 15–16
bezel (compass), 34, 43–44

Big Dipper, 18–19
blazes, 72–73
boulders, navigating, 81
boxing the needle, 44–45
breaks, taking, 84–85
Brunton, 34, 38, 44, 50–51, 166–168
Brunton-Resync, 167
Bureau of Land Management, 68–69
Bureau of Land Management maps, 2, 183

cairns, 73
camping, xiii–xiv, 71–72
cardinal directions, 6
Casio, 93
catching features, 76
color systems, maps, 9–10, 174
compass(es). *See also specific parts of*
    calibrating, 38
    cardinal directions on, 6
    declination adjustment, 36
    defined, 32
    dependency on, 1, 31–32
    history of the, 32
    magnets and, 40–41, 125
    for open space routefinding, 82
    orienting maps with/without, 17–21, 46–47

parts of, 33–34, 43–45, 52–53, 125
travel and, 36–37, 39–40
types of, 33, 35, 37–39
compass bearings, 47–52, 83–84
compass dip, 40
compass errors, 40–41
compass rulers, 34
computers for navigation, 128, 151–157. *See also* tablet computers
contouring, 85–86
contour intervals, 9, 13
contour lines, 4, 10, 12–13, 15–17, 21–25
converging contours, 13
coordinates/coordinate systems, 9, 101–103, 114–115
COSPAS, 139
COSPAS-SARSAT satellite system, 139–142

Dakota GPS handheld, 158
datum settings, 121–122
declination, 42–44
declination adjustment, 36
declination diagrams, 9, 43–44, 47
degrees, minutes, seconds, 34, 108, 122
Delorme, 143, 144, 146, 156, 158
deserts, navigating, 82–83
direction-of-travel arrow, 34, 45, 47
distance, estimating and measuring, 11–12, 36, 84–85, 89–90
drainages, 15–16, 82

Earth
latitude/longitude coordinate system, 108
magnetic properties of, 32, 39–40

primary and optional zones, 103–104
shape of the, 121
Earthmate PN-60w, 158
easting values, 105
elevation, 41, 160. *See also* altimeters
elevation gains, measuring, 24–25
e-mail, emergency, 142, 143
emergency beacons, 138–146

Fast Find PLB, 141–142
fires when lost, 149
Fusil, Gerard, 177

game trails, 74
Garmin, 93, 158
gear, essential, xii
geocaching, 124, 130–131
glaciers and glacial till, 10, 81–82
global pivot, 36–37
Globalstar, 143, 145
GLONASS, 117
Goal Zero, 167–168
Google AR, 163–165
Google Earth, 140, 156
Google maps, 144, 162, 164
Goto function, 124–125
GPS-based altimeters, 91–92, 96
GPS (global positioning system), 82, 116–120, 139–140, 159–162
GPS handheld receivers
buying, 120, 126–129
operating a, 121–126
preloaded maps on, 155–156
skills practice, 129–131
smartphones vs., 157–158
grades, 22, 24
grids on maps, 101–102, 113
guidebook maps, 2, 4

gunsight notch, 52–53
gyroscope, 161

handrails, routefinding using, 76
headlamps, 168
housing (compass), 34

ice fields, navigating, 82–83
index contours, 13
index line, 34, 44, 47
inReach, 144
intermediate contours, 13

Joos, 167
Juice Pack Pro, 170

lanyard (compass), 36
latitude/longitude coordinate sys-
    tem, 102, 108–114, 122
Leave No Trace principles, xiii–xv
line features, 76
line position, 58–60
log cuts, 73
lost
    admitting you are, 133–136
    emergency beacons, 138–146
    planning to avoid getting, 134,
        150
    searching for people who are,
        146–150
    what to do when, 135–139

magnetic dip zones, 39–40
magnetic north, 42–44, 47
magnets and compasses, 40–41,
    125

magnifying glass (compass), 36–37
map(s). See also quads (USGS
    quadrangle maps); topo
    (topographic) maps; specific
    types of
    choosing, 2–5
    color system, 9–10, 174
    distance on, 11–12
    online resources for, 183
    orienting, 17–21, 46–47, 86–88
    outside North America, 39–40
    weatherproofing, 5, 183
map cases, 5
map display on GPS receivers,
    128–129
map markings, 10, 15–16, 43,
    101–102, 108–109, 113–114
mapping software, 151–157, 161,
    170–171
map rulers, 103, 111
marshes, 10
McMurdo, 141–142
meridians, 34, 111
metric-English measurement con-
    version, 90
metric/statute distances, 122
minutes, seconds, and degrees,
    108, 122
Montana GPS handheld, 158
Mophie Juice Pack Pro, 170
mountains, 15–16, 21–24, 71, 91,
    97–98

National Geographic Society, 5,
    156, 162
National Geographic Trails, 183
National Oceanic and Atmos-
    pheric Association (NOAA),
    139, 143
National Park Service (NPS), 68
National Park Service (NPS) maps,
    2, 183

navigation
   apps for, 159–166
   competitive, 172–179
   defined, xi
   the sun and stars for, 17–20,
      83–84
needle (compass), 33–34, 44–45,
   125
nighttime travel, 17–21, 31, 51–53,
   83–84, 137–138, 164, 176
north, 17–20, 32
northing values, 105
North Star (Polaris), 18–19
notches, 16–17

obstacles, going around, 48–50
off- and on-trail travel, 70–78, 87
open space, navigating, 82–83
Oregon GPS handheld, 158
orientation, defined, xi
orienteering, xi, 172–175, 184
orienteering maps, 174
orienting arrow, 34, 36, 43–44

pace, counting and setting, 84–85,
   89
pace meter, 89
pan track, 125–126
parallels, 109
passes, 16–17
peep sight, 52–53
personal locator beacons (PLBs),
   138–146
photovoltaic panels (PVs), 166
planimetric maps, 2, 4
planning and preparation. *See also*
   batteries
   to avoid getting lost, 134, 150
   essentials, xi–xiii
   nighttime travel, 83–84
   terrain association in, 13–17
   for time and effort, 24–25

travel plans, xii, 25–28
   when lost, 149
Point Last Seen (PLS), 147–148
position format and fix, 122–123
prismatic compass, 36
private land, tresspassing on,
   69–70
public lands, 68–70, 180–181, 183

quads (USGS quadrangle maps),
   4–10, 43, 47, 102–106,
   113–114, 122, 151. *See also*
   map(s)

rangefinders, 164
recreation maps, 2
reentrants, 15–16
reference altitude, 94
relief maps, 5
ResQLink PLB, 141–142
ridges, 15–16, 82
rock cairns, 73
rocks, falling, 21–22
rogaining, 172, 175–176, 184
routefinding. *See also specific*
   terrain
   average speed, 88–90
   cautions, 70, 80
   contouring, 85–86
   defined, xi
   errors, 66–68, 87
   maps and, 86–88
   nighttime travel, 31, 83–84
   off- and on-trail, 70–78, 87
   pace setting/pace counting,
      84–85
   on private land, 69–70
   skills practice, 87–90, 184
Rugged Outdoor Group Activity
   Involving Navigation and
   Endurance (ROGAINE), 175

saddles, 16–17
satellite communicators, 138–146
scale, 4, 12–13, 22, 29, 39, 103, 106, 108, 174–175
scree, navigating, 81
search and rescue (SAR), 138, 143, 149–150
see, 74–75
shot, 74–75
sidehilling, 86
sighting mirrors, 34, 36, 52–53
signal mirrors, 149
Silva, 38, 44, 93
slope gauges, 22–23
slopes, 21–22
smart-GPS, 157–158
smartphones
    altimeters on, 96
    apps for navigation, 159–162
    batteries and portable power for, 165–171
    with compasses, 38
    GPS on, 117, 120–121, 126, 128–129, 141, 143–144, 146, 157–158
Solaris 4 Panel, 167
solar power, 166–167
Southern Cross, 19
speed of travel, calculating, 84–85, 88–90, 130
SPOT, 139, 143–146
spurs, 15–16
statute distances, 122
steep terrain, 13, 21–24, 78–80, 86
summit, defined, 15
survey lines, 10
Suunto, 38, 50–51, 93

tablet computers, 129, 146, 151, 153, 157–158, 159–160, 165–171. *See also* computers for navigation

talus, navigating, 81
technology. *See also specific types of*
    future of, 181–182
    relying on, xv, 1–2, 96, 116, 153–154, 170–171
    temperature and, 41, 93–95, 160, 170
terrain, classes of (YDS), 78–80
terrain association, 1, 4, 13–17, 20–21, 28–29, 32, 52–53, 58–60
text messages, 142, 143, 145, 146, 158
theodolites, 163
three-dimensional maps, 5
thumb compass, 51
thumbing, 86–87
Times digital altimeters, 93
topo (topographic) maps, 3–6, 39, 43, 174, 183. *See also* map(s); quads (USGS quadrangle maps)
topo (topographic) map software, 151–157
township and range grid system, 10, 113–114
track-back, 125–126
trail markers and numbers, 10, 72–73
trails, xiii
tresspassing, 69–70
triangulating, 58–60
true north, 6, 43, 44–45

United States Geological Survey (USGS), 4–5
Universal Transverse Mercator (TM) coordinate system, 9, 102–108, 114, 122
Universal Transverse Mercator (TM) grid readers, 106
US Fish and Wildlife Service (USFWS), 69

US Forest Service (USFS), 69, 183
US Geological Survey Map Store,
    183

weather, 5, 94–96, 98–99, 183. *See
    also* temperature *under* tech-
    nology
whistles, 137
Wilderness Act, 69

Wilderness Study Areas (WSAs),
    69
wilderness travel
    additional resources, 184–185
    Leave No Trace principles, xiii–xv
wrist-top GPS receivers, 127–128

Yosemite Decimal System (YDS),
    78–80